# WHEN EGO DIES

## A Compilation of Near-Death & Mystical Conversion Experiences

Foreword by Diane K. Corcoran, RN, Ph.D.

*A book by and for recycled souls*

## EMERALD INK
PUBLISHING

Library of Congress Cataloging-in-Publication Data
When ego dies: a compilation of near-death & mystical conversion
  experiences / foreword by Diane K. Corcoran.
      p. cm.
    Includes bibliograpphical references and index.
    ISBN 1-885373-07-4
    1. Near-death experiences. 2. Course in miracles. 3. Mysticism.
  1. Emerald Ink Publishing.
  BF1045.N4W44 1996
  133.9'01'3--dc20
96-10140

Printed in the United States of America

BOOK DESIGN BY J.K. BAREFIELD

Angel illustration by Houston area illustrator Lani Anderson

"The effects of meeting truth are profound: one's thinking and eventually one's life change at death. This effect of experiencing truth sets the meeting of the Light apart from other phenomena people attribute to the near death experience — drug trips, hallucinations, oxygen deprivation, massive endorphin releases, stress, memory of birth trauma and so on. However, these other experiences do not change lives permanently.

And yet there are people who cannot let peace break out. They still try to prove that this most powerful experience is just some little side effect of physical life sputtering out. This silly straining against a higher consciousness, even if it could prove something, says nothing about the millions of experiences occurring without any hint of physical death.

'...experiencers may try to hide it, even from themselves.'

If it is not only death that causes these occurrences, what is the cause? Though death is not a prerequisite, some kind of physical or emotional trauma is generally present. A devastating emotional, mental or religious disappointment that can trigger it.

Sometimes experiencers think they have been given a job to accomplish on earth but they can't remember what it was.

When their stories are told in group, the sincerity is palpable and the effects are very healing on even the non-experiencers in the group."

P. M. H. Atwater, author of *Beyond the Light:*
*What Isn't Being Said About the Near-Death Experience*

# • D E D I C A T I O N •

This book is dedicated to the experiencers and interested supporters who made this collection of stories possible.

They contributed their time and exerted the effort to write their very personal disclosures. They willingly laid themselves open emotionally to explain to others what they felt, thought and believed in the most important event in their lives. They have tried to show the readers how important it is to communicate, to share and to love those around you, now and forever.

All the contributors fervently hope that their efforts will assist others in giving up fear of life as well as fear of death. Turn the page and your life will change, too.

# TABLE OF CONTENTS

# • A c k n o w l e d g m e n t s •

P. M. H. Atwater

Diane Corcoran, Ph.D.

Max Washburn

J. K. Barefield

Bill Bingham

Carole Jarrett

Jack Jarrett

Dennis Ivy

Patrick Zale

Nathan Gatch

Ronald Thibeaux

Marguerite & Paul Carson

Judith Sheffield

Lani Anderson

This book is ecologically correct: written, photographed and published by recycled souls on recycled paper.

# • F O R E W O R D •

*Lt. Col. Diane Corcoran, RN, Ph.D., Nursing Management Consultant, 1st Vice President of IANDS, details her emergent involvement with the Near-Death (and related) experiences.*

What is it like to die?

Most of us really can't say for sure despite what has been written for centuries by scientists, poets, novelists and those who think they know. Yet millions of people living in all parts of the world have had *Near-Death Experiences* (*NDEs*) which seem to provide fascinating glimpses of the other side. Many of these *experiencers* have shared their personal events with us, true gifts of sharing.

This book is all about sharing and giving. Some people have been reliving their NDE over and over but some have been unable to talk about it, and finally they share their experiences here. This book is about not feeling alone; it is about giving information, time and suggestions on how to find other people who understand their experiences and how to follow their new perceptions of their world and their new paths in life.

Although I have not had a Near-Death Experience, two encounters with NDE experiencers have significantly changed the way I look at living and dying. These two encounters have changed the way I look at grieving, the way I work with the dying and the way I live my personal and professional life. The first encounter was in 1976 when my father had an NDE while being resuscitated from a cardiac arrest, and the second encounter was in 1980 with a 26 year old terminal cancer patient I was working with in Fort Hood, Texas.

My father was a very quiet, well-grounded man who didn't believe in anything paranormal. Yet this experience consumed him, an experience he shared with me as soon as he could talk. He was never afraid of dying after his NDE.

This event led me to the university library where I was doing my doctoral work. I took on the arduous task of finding any literature on the subject. This search was a difficult journey which led me around the world, back to the beginning of time, through mental health and religious literature and eventually to Raymond Moody's book, *Life After Life*. He is the author who defined the phenomenon as the Near-Death Experience (NDE). This search also led me to my long involvement with the International Association of Near-Death Studies (IANDS), and to my many friendships and professional relationships with some of the most knowledgeable people I know. All of these events helped when my dad had a stroke in 1994.

In his final days, I used his memory of this experience to free him from his tortured body and lovingly told him to once again find the light, peace and contentment of the other side.

Debra, the second person placed in my path who had had an NDE, was petrified of the entire concept of dying. I was then an evening and night supervisor of Darnell Army Hospital at Ft. Hood, Texas, where during this time I was doing some additional work as the Army's version of hospice, and was referred to many of the terminal patients. Debra was assigned to me after she had been given her diagnosis of terminal lung cancer. We quickly began to work on some of her issues. We talked for hours about dying. I did not share my new-found knowledge of NDEs with her at that time for the NDE was not a commonly-known phenomenon, and at that point I had not considered using it with terminal patients. I worked with Debra for months, but we were unable to progress much because she was petrified with the thought of dying. Yet Debra was soon to change both of our lives forever. During a critical event where she had a respiratory arrest in the ambulance, she had an NDE. By the time she reached the hospital, not only was she breathing again, she was also filled with joy, had resolved all her fears of dying and was basking in a state of contentment.

However, this was short-lived as she tried to explain to her doctor what had happened. He proceeded to tell her that she was having a psychotic reaction to medication, for he had no understanding of her experience. This, of course, immediately deflated her sense of peace and contentment. She became angry at this physician who had dared to infer that she was crazy. By now she knew that I would listen and that I would be able to reassure her on her mental status, so she called me. Because of my father's NDE, I had read extensively about the topic and I felt free to share with Debra and her family the information that I had gathered over the previous years. Debra died two days later. As she slipped contentedly over to the other side, unbeknownst to me, she had left me with a mission to fulfill. Before she left, she thanked me for providing her with support during the dying process and for the information and guidance I had given her about the Near-Death Experience. At last she knew her sanity was intact. Therefore, Debra's last moments had been of contentment, peace and closeness with her family.

Debra's final request before she died was for me to not let her doctor or any other provider's lack of information hurt other patients as it had hurt her. She wanted to be reassured of my commitment in the teaching of health care professionals to prevent future NDE experiencers from being emotionally and spiritually traumatized by those who instead should assure their patient's well-being, care and comfort.

These encounters happened many years ago. Ever since, I have been teaching and lecturing to the healthcare system and to many provider organizations. I have incorporated this perspective of my life and death into all aspects of my life. I have even introduced corporate America to the NDE during brown bag lunches and personal discussions. It is amazing that even in that environment, so many people have come back to me for information after learning that a family member or friend was also an NDE experiencer.

*When Ego Dies* is a book about listening, teaching and healing. I trust that the experiencers in this book will feel some healing effects by just sharing their stories. The book is also an excellent resource for other experiencers, their families and those interested in learning from the experts what it feels like to die and how it might impact on the rest of one's life.

I have used my work with experiencers as a framework for treating many patients. I use the NDE information in grief work, with terminal patients, with SIDS babies, with AIDS patients, and with the families and friends of those who are dying. It is also my observation that people who have lost a loved one frequently benefit from knowing about the Near-Death Experience.

It gives them new alternatives to consider when thinking about where their loved ones are or how they are feeling. Nothing takes all the pain of losing someone go away, but many people have written and told me how much better they have felt knowing that there may be something on the other side. The book *When Ego Dies* provides many different perspectives and alternatives when looking at death.

*When Ego Dies* is very straightforward. It tells the truth of each person's understanding of their own experience. It also gives readers resources such as:

> •**International Association of Near-Death Studies** (IANDS)[1], the *only* organization solely dedicated to the support, teaching and research in the field of Near-Death Studies. This book is also an excellent resource for those who truly want to hear how the experiencer feels and what he sees during his or her experience.
>
> •**Spiritual Frontiers Fellowship International**[2] which studies the relationship of the NDE with world religions and sacred traditions.

Near-Death Experiences can happen to anyone around the world. However, in many cases, the experiencer is not familiar with the short or long term impact of the event, let alone how to integrate it into daily life.

Anyone in search of becoming a better-informed person in the field of NDEs can use *When Ego Dies* for its quality information. Most experiencers are not looking for a cure, nor an explanation, but just for a loving person who will listen.

There are many loving people who have shared their stories here and many resources so none of you have to feel alone or without help. *When Ego Dies* gives each of you a chance to hear just how often this wondrous trip happens and provides a guide to many helping hearts.

---

1  IANDS, P. O. Box 502, East Windsor Hill, CT 06028-0502 USA. (203) 528-5144.

2  Spiritual Frontiers Fellowship International, P.O. Box 7868 Philadelphia, PA. 19101-7868 (215) 222-1991.

*Diane K. Corcoran has lived a successful life as a Lt. Colonel in the US Army, an RN, a Ph.D. and 1st Vice President of IANDS. She has been written about in such publications as "On Call" about glimpses of eternity and tirelessly speaks to medical professionals and the general public on the implications of the NDE.*

*Diane K. Corcoran, RN, Ph.D.*

# The Truth about the Light

This is a book about the greatest and most important experience of a lifetime, a near death experience (NDE) or spiritual conversion experience.

The experiencers themselves share, in their own words, their encounters of the Light. They speak from their highest truth. These encounters with the Light establish what is the truth for them.

The mystic sages of the ancient faiths, when asked about truth, often said "If you *think* it is truth, it is not." When truth shows up, you will *know* it. Einstein knew how little we really know with our brain and how much there is to know. He said:

> *"My religious feeling consists in a humble admiration for the infinitely superior spirit manifesting itself in the little reality that we are able to recognize with our weakened frail reason."*[1]

An experiencer of the light *know*s his truth. William James said it well in his landmark turn-of-the-century book, ***Varieties of Religious Experience***: "Mysticism is self-certifying because it is a form of knowledge so personal as to be beyond words."

Some twenty years after my experience I was introduced to three books (now combined into one) called ***A Course In Miracles***. I've been attending *A Course In Miracles* study group every week in the fourteen years since. The popularity of this material has gone way beyond the wildest expectations of the Ph.D. psychologists who wrote down these illuminations.

---

1   Einstein to M. M. Schayer, 8/5/27, Einstein Archives.

Because historically some channelers have proven to be less than clean, I am reluctant to use the word 'channeled' in connection with the *Course in Miracles* without some explanation. 'Channeled' is a more descriptive word than 'written' and connotes superior communication from a higher consciousness translated accurately and faithfully to voice or paper.

It's a pity how so many egos react negatively to that word, especially since, if we reflect a moment, we will know that much, if not all of the world's great art, music, literature — and yes, even science — have been channeled. Einstein took a nap every day. He felt it was conducive to inspiration. The Webster dictionary defines the word *inspire* as "...to cause, guide, communicate or motivate as by divine or supernatural influence." Newton checked with a higher power regularly.

The Koran, said to be the revealed word of Allah, the one God to the world's second largest religion, was 'channeled' by Mohammed over a period of 22 years! Incidentally, the name of that religion, Islam, means 'surrender'. Surrender by ego is the key to the NDE.

Many of the great artists have fessed up to it; the composers say it best:

*"When in my most inspired moods, I have definite compelling visions involving a higher selfhood. I feel at such moments that I am tapping the source of infinite and eternal energy from which you and I and all things proceed. Religion calls it God." (Richard Strauss)*

*"I have very definite impressions while in that trancelike condition, which is the prerequisite of all true creative effort. I feel that I am one with this vibrating Force that is omniscient, and that I can draw upon it by an intent that is limited only by my own capacity to do so." (Wagner)*

*"We composers are projectors of the infinite into the finite. "(Grieg)*[2]

The scribes of *A Course in Miracles* thought it might appeal to a few dozen people. I understand that now more than one million copies are in print. As you will see in my experience, I had

---

2  Godwin, Jocelyn. *Harmonies of Heaven and Earth*. Rochester, VT: Inner Traditions Int., Ltd. 1987.

some illuminations regarding forgiveness and acceptance. These are the bottom-line functional principals in *A Course In Miracles.* I also see in the course how all the important epiphanies of my life fit into a continuous, complete thought system. Before *A Course in Miracles,* they seemed disjointed, possibly related only on some much higher plane than human thought. As far as words can go, the course expresses beautifully in flavor and content some of the knowledge fallout from my experience. I quote freely from the course:

> *"Truth can only be experienced. It cannot be described and it cannot be explained."3*

We find similar tenets in Buddhism, Taoism and Hinduism. The effects of meeting truth are profound: one's thinking and eventually one's life change at depth. This effect of experiencing truth sets the meeting of the Light apart from other phenomena people attribute the near death experience to: drug trips, hallucinations, oxygen deprivation, massive endorphin releases, stress, memory of birth trauma and so on. These other experiences do not change lives permanently. They do not relieve people of the fear of death as the NDE does. *A Course In Miracles* says it well:

> *"In the presence of truth, there are no unbelievers and no sacrifices. In the security of reality, fear is meaningless."4*

And yet there are people who cannot let peace break out. They still try to prove that this most powerful experience is just some little side effect of physical life sputtering out. This silly straining against a higher consciousness, even if it could prove something, says nothing about the millions of mystical conversion experiences occurring without any hint of physical death.

At any rate, modern science has drastically revised our notion of the physical: that which used to be considered solid matter—even at the subatomic particle level—is not solid. Everything is a form of energy and that energy thinks: it behaves intelligently. So scientists have proven what Buddha knew 3000 years ago when he said "Everything is mind."

---

3  *A Course in Miracles*, 1975, Chapter 8, The Treasure of God.
4  *A Course in Miracles*, Chapter 9, The Acceptance of Reality.

Science has shifted from discrete atomism to field theory as a basis for fundamental reality. This speaks of the fundamental relatedness of all things!

Could it be that at bodily death, our limited little consciousnesses move to that perspective "reality" where all consciousnesses are connected? And what a joyous reunion it is. Could the light be pure consciousness? Maybe more? Most experiencers feel that truth! The opening to the Tibetan Book of the Dead states:

*"To the Divine Body of Truth the Incomprehensible Boundless Light."*

Although the experiencers' thinking changes radically and immediately, their outward lives sometimes take years to change. They often tend not to talk about the experience at first, even trying to suppress the existence of the experience. In my NDE support group, we hear:

*"People might think I was crazy"*

*"I tried telling people but nobody wants to hear it"*

*"People close to me seem threatened by it"*

*"I tried to tell my minister/priest about it but he only wanted to know if I saw hell"*

*"My minister just kept asking me what I thought about faith. He couldn't see how it was different from faith, that I had a memory of something that actually happened to me that was much more profound than anything ever in my life."*

So experiencers may try to hide it, even from themselves. But a big change has occurred in their psyche and it cannot be denied. Eventually the change shows up in their external lives. The content of this experience feels much more real than what passes for reality in everyday life. It feels like home, the home of all homes. It feels like the way life ought to be and we know could be. We also know that is the way it will be after the death of this suit of clothes that we call our body. So we don't fear death.

*"The sage does not fear death. Too often had he died to ego and its vanities, to all that keeps man tied."* (Selisius)[5]

---

5  *The Book of Angelus Selisius*, p. 74.

My words can't do the slightest justice to the experience—
no words can. The words that come closest I've seen in 33 years
of reading on the subject are those of Angelus Selisius. Born
Johannes Scheffler in 17th century Germany, he was a medical
doctor who had a profound four day experience of the light. He
is very germane to our purpose because he recorded in wonderful, terse poetry his insights *during* his illumination.

The loss of the fear of death is a universal attribute of the
experience, one of the few universals of the experience. The
details of these experiences can vary widely, far from the "stan-
dardized" television version which is as follows:

A person dies on the operating table. He perceives his body
from a remote location, goes through a dark tunnel at a great
speed, meets a being of light, feels wonderful, returns to life,
rests in love and wisdom ever after.

The loss of the fear of death, the great awe of it all and the
ensuing life changes may be the only universal aspects of the
most profound transformational experiences.

We know that a person does not have to die for the experience to occur. After my experience, I was drawn to the teachings
of Buddhism, Taoism and Hinduism. These great traditions
emphasize direct and profound experience of a higher power or
principle in everyday living, not only in dying. I identified with
the feelings, visions and effects of the powerful mystical conversions related in these traditions.

Many years later when I read *Life After Life* by Dr. Raymond
Moody, I totally identified again. I saw that NDE's were the
same as experiences of the ancient and modern mystics. Moody
even mentions the story from the Bible of Paul's mystical conversion on the road to Damascus as a precedent for the Near-
Death Experience.

The Bible tells of many mystical conversions when a person's life changes radically to focus on God after a traumatic
experience other than death. This is not generally emphasized in
the Christian churches. You have to discover the writings of the
great Christian mystics such as Meister Eckhardt, Jacob Boeme,
William Blake, St. John of the Cross and others for yourself.
Dying is not a standard part of receiving this type of experience.

In 1982, George Gallup, Jr. published a book called *Adventures in Immortality*. After surveying thousands of experiences, he found that only a small percentage have a tunnel or out-of-body experience.

The stories you will read in this book are told from the highest truth of the heart, not the intellect. The details vary widely but the deeply moving effects of the ego-overpowering feelings of ecstatic joy and love are evident in all.

If it is not only death that causes these occurrences, what is the cause? Though death is not a prerequisite, some kind of physical or emotional trauma is generally present. A devastating emotional, mental or religious disappointment can trigger it. In the many hundreds of stories that I have read or heard in my NDE and Mystical Experience support group, I notice a point of surrender that immediately precedes the spiritual part of the experience. It occurs as the ego gives up trying to control and the spirit sings out, as a caged bird might if given freedom.

I feel that in physical death the ego dies because as *A Course In Miracles* says "... ego is of the body... Ego is a thought of fear." But I know that ego can also be temporarily set aside in other traumatic ways: the intense practice of Zen Buddhism is a direct attack on the ego. The Roshi may never say so. However, it is evident in the koans, verbal puzzles designed to blow the literal, reductionistic mind away.

The attack is especially evident in the marathon *Zen* sessions; sitting in meditation seventeen hours a day for seven days will create very severe physical pain, crushing boredom and emotional anguish at the least. This is most of what Zen is about—much practice, some teaching. Though the Zen circumstances are such that ego thinks it will surely deserve great shame if it quits, it finally says "I can't handle any more of this."

Amazingly, at that instant, pain, boredom and anguish disappear. Euphoria, bliss and joy arise. Not a hair has moved, ego surrendered — that is all. Only awe can be the state of mind at this time. Later, as thinking arises, euphoria collapses at the instant ego takes credit for it—a very powerful lesson in what and where pain is.

*"Until you lose your Me you cannot see God's face—the moment you recover it you fall from Grace."[6]*

I feel that ego death (or at least unconditional temporary surrender) rests at the bottom of Near Death Experience, Kundalini Rising and mystical experiences of all kinds. Of course, our egos eventually reinstate themselves but they have been permanently altered. Since ego is mainly about fear, loss of fear of death has weakened it considerably. The memory of the overpowering feelings of unconditional love while encountering the light constantly remind us of the prime importance and reality of love.

Love is another strong ego-diminishing power. The Bible says,

*"Perfect love casts out all fear."[7]*

The strongest and most consistent messages reported by experiencers are:

*"What is most important in life is love and learning"* and

*"You don't have to fear death. There is a better life beyond."*

I feel that even the learning has to do with love; learning to remove the blocks to love, as *A Course in Miracles* says:

*"The course does not aim at teaching the meaning of love, for that is beyond what can be taught. It does aim, however, at removing the blocks to the awareness of love's presence, which is your natural inheritance. The opposite of love is fear, but what is all-encompassing can have no opposite."[8]*

Selisius relates love to death of the body beautifully:

*"Love is like death—it kills the self-willed Me. It breaks its stranglehold and sets the Spirit free."[9]*

However, all may not be bliss ever after for the experiencer. Some classic mystical experience survivors remain dysfunctional for years, among them Gopi Krishna for twelve years and Walt Whitman. As the awe and afterglow begin to wear off, the experiencer may feel serious frustration with the mundane world he now faces, irritated by the pettiness and fear that he now sees

---

6  *The Book of Angelus Selisius* p 45.
7  John, Chapter 4, verse 18.
8  *A Course in Miracles*, Introduction.
9  *The Book of Angelus Selisius*, p 74.

is so rampant in everyday life. He sees how people get in the way of their own happiness. He loves more but his love may not be as recognizable to those close to him. The love is less possessive and codependent, more *laissez-faire*, more broadly bestowed. He is more sensitive to all people. He may be more intuitive and psychic. The new-found abilities can cause problems too if not properly handled. Physical sensitivities of many kinds may appear as an aftereffect.

Many experiencers recall that at some point they were given the meaning of life but they cannot now formulate or remember what that was. They were "...not allowed to bring it back." This too is frustrating. My personal memory of this "all-knowing" was not that universal. I knew everything about whatever individual thing I focused attention on. If I focused on a cat, I saw every atom in its body. I knew its history, perspective on life, place in the universe and so on. This description gives a sense of what I knew. It is not exactly how it was. We are in a consciousness where words fail. We are way beyond literal, even linguistic brain function. As the Upanishad says:

*"Realizing that from which all words turn back and thoughts can never reach, one knows the bliss of Brahman and fears no more."*[10]

In these mystical experiences, the mind has been set free. It has much greater powers of observation, collation and comprehension than when encumbered by the demands of every day senses and functions. Without these expanded powers, it is difficult if not impossible to remember and translate and connect the details, nuances and even meanings of what was experienced.

Sometimes experiencers think they have been given a job to accomplish on earth but they can't remember what it was. The effects of this experience continue to mature over time and will last at least a lifetime. The driving quest to find this job can be frustrating and sometimes tragic.

When their stories are told in group, the sincerity is palpable and the effects are very healing on even the non-experiencers in the group. The stories are especially healing for the teller and other experiencers, but in different ways; the non-experiencers

---

10 Taittiriya Upanishad, Sect 4.1, Black Yajur Veda.

can lose some of their fear of death and therefore fear of life. They may be comforted that departed or departing loved ones have a place to go, at least in consciousness. The experiencers get healing in revealing what to them is their highest truth. They may not have many people or any at home that they can talk to about the experience of a higher power.

These experiences cry out to be shared! They come from a place in the heart-mind that *knows* this is where mankind should live; this is where we will live if we are to progress and not just be annihilated. Humanity is a movement—a movement of being. Its seed was in the big bang; it has climbed up out of the sea to the tree tops then to the skyscrapers. It is now struggling to a new height of higher consciousness. The struggle, which is evolution, has always been on the field of consciousness. Giving birth to this truly New Age "New Paradigm" will be painful. All true birth, true creation is painful and frustrating but well worth it. Spiritual consciousness cannot die. The birth of its full awareness in human consciousness will be infinitely worth the struggle. This higher consciousness is a giant step above the kill-for-food consciousness out of which our physical nature grew and our competitive kill-or-be-killed attitude that keeps so much fear in place today.

We hope that these stories will bring some healing of old fears and worries to you.

*Bill Bingham, Experiencer*

*"Love's power to restore the broken shards into one whole is the supreme attainment of the human soul."[11]*

---

11 *The Book of Angelus Silesius.*

*Bill Bingham has been studying the great religions of the world and practising many of their techniques and precepts since his experience 34 years ago. While alone one afternoon, he was totally and permanently transformed from a doubting agnostic to a knower of certainty of a higher power and eternal life. Long retired from making a living, he facilitates a Near-Death and Mystical Experiences Support Group in Houston, Texas. He feels that if there were a curriculum for these experiences in every school, there would be a whole lot less fear and a great deal more love in the world.*

# $\mathscr{T}$he NDE From an Observer's Viewpoint

My husband and I have been involved with this NDE group from its inception. We were friends with Max Washburn, a founder, and I offered my computer skills to help with recording keeping, lists of attendees, mailing, etc.

My husband Jack and I have been interested in metaphysics for many years and had a curiosity about near-death experiences since reading Raymond Moody's book *Life After Life*. Never having had an NDE, I bring a different viewpoint to this book.

The most interesting thing to me is the enormous divergence in beliefs this group has. Most have had a paranormal experience of some type, either NDE's or mystical conversion experiences, as some choose to call them. There seem to be different motivations for the people who come who are not experiencers. Occasionally a person, or couple, will come who have lost a child. They seem to find the stories of the experiencers comforting and useful to their healing process. Others, like my husband and I, are curious and looking for answers for ourselves. The common experiences of these people are impressive for searchers who would rather listen to those who are speaking from their own knowledge and experience rather than those who are passing down a belief system, often based on fear of disbelief, without any experience to confirm those beliefs.

The beliefs range from fundamental Christians with strong beliefs in Heaven, Hell and judgment, to strong metaphysical beliefs in reincarnation, karma, and continuing evolution. The common results of these experiences seem to be a certain knowledge that the soul survives death, loss of fear of death, changed lives, and belief in a loving higher power.

The discussions get heated sometimes, but people are polite and seem to be respectful of different belief systems.

Being what I would call a *truth seeker*, I find this lack of consensus rather frustrating, but it also confirms my belief that the TRUTH is not knowable from this perspective. Even those people who seem very evolved spiritually and have knowledge gained through meditation and other extrasensory means do not always agree on what they know.

Despite so many people believing they know the Truth, most of them will disagree on what it is — Christian, Muslim, Buddhist, Hindu. To me, this confirms the idea that the truth is not knowable from this perspective. If it were, there would only be one belief system whose truth would be obvious to everyone. No one argues the answers in math, and other sciences have provable positions. Only religion seems to evoke such strong belief given such lack of provable consistency in individual beliefs. Some experiencers seem to have found their truth though they now have more questions than answers. It may take lifetimes to get all the answers. Where experiencers disagree is in the interpretations of what they experienced.

I don't believe a just and loving God could give each soul only one lifetime, as unequal as they obviously are, and judge that soul based on the outcome of that life. Reincarnation was a part of the Bible until the Council of Nicea in 325 CE when it was removed.

The lives look rather predetermined to me, especially if one is required to be a Christian to be saved, or any other religion for that matter. Most people are raised to believe in the religion of their family and the people around them, and conversion is not an option for most who strongly believe their way is the right way, unless they have had an experience that has made them more open minded and less sure of their previous belief system.

I would hope readers of this book will find in the NDE experiences described here answers to their questions about the afterlife and the loving Creator of us all.

*Carole Jarrett*

# mazement

*Melanie Baldwin, a civil engineer in Houston, tells her story.*

I was given anesthesia for an operation. Apparently I was given too much—the next thing I remembered after being put to sleep was being conscious and moving feet first down a tunnel at an enormous speed. I was aware that I was on my way to somewhere but I did not know where. I noticed bright lights of all different colors that seemed to stream by because I was moving so fast. It would be similar to being a particle on a stream of light (being an engineer I know light moves at an enormous speed. As I moved further along I became aware of a bright— extremely white—light. The moment I became aware of the light, I automatically began communicating. I became aware of where I was moving to at such a high speed. I began communicating telepathically that I did not want to go now, that I wanted to go back. I repeated this idea as I became closer and closer. The light radiated an extreme feeling of love, it was overwhelming. I could tell I had been there before and was so happy to be going home. The closer I came, the happier I was and the more I anticipated being home. The knowledge of the light knew me totally. The communication was simultaneous and sharing. It was similar to a feeling of arriving home in your driveway or city, when you have been gone for a long, long time, and you can't wait to run into the house and see your family and loved ones. This feeling, but intensified greatly! I felt my heart would burst with joy and happiness. At this same instant I knew this light contained great knowledge. For that moment I became one with the light. The communication was like talking with your mother or father who was all loving and had all knowledge, and only wanted what was best, but at the same time there was a great magnitude of attraction to the light, it was pulling me towards it. I knew that was where I belonged and I would be returning.

Since we were one, the decision was made jointly that I would return. It was my desire, and also there was one person who would have blamed themselves for my death.

I returned instantaneously to my body, This experience was like being reborn. I felt I was experiencing my body for the first time. I very slowly began moving each finger and staring with amazement. I proceeded to slowly take control of each part of my body. When I was fully conscious, I was very thankful to have my life again. Immediately after this experience, I felt very alive, I sensed the life in everything. Each blade of grass seemed to be alive and full of energy.

Since that experience, I have looked upon life with more love and understanding. I know there is great loving power— "God"—who is always with each of us. We will all return to our light of love. I also try daily to help others and to reflect the love and understanding that I felt. I believe that if we all knew, where we came from and where we are going to return, we would be more loving, peaceful and knowledgeable as a country and as a universe.

*Melanie Baldwin*

# Near Death Experience

*Retired from nursing and running children's shoe stores, Lonnie McDougle served on the Board of Directors and as Volunteer Coordinator of Triangle AIDS Network. She is currently devoting full time to nursing son Rick on his own AIDS journey.*

My son Rick was climbing up the side of one of the teenagers forming a pyramid of muscular young men, all showing off in the Sabine River one sunny Saturday.

I stood in the water nearby, shading my eyes with one hand, and gesturing to Rick as I encouraged him on his way to the top, He was one excited twelve-year-old as he made the first shoulder, and began climbing the second layer.

When I backed up to get a better perspective, I stepped down and down on nothing but water. My other foot slipped on the sandy bottom, and I plopped under water. Just as quickly, I popped up to the surface, and the young man my son had just climbed said, "Hey, what's happening?"

I laughed. Nervously I laughed and said, "I can't swim." Then I sank again, this time telling myself, "Don't open your mouth. Just keep slowly breathing out your nose and you won't strangle on water. Slow-breathe-out, slow-breathe out." All the while we moved with the water, not struggling.'Twas the truth, I really couldn't swim.

I must have sunk like a brick. I wasn't surprised at the darkness. Keeping water out of my eyes was an automatic response. Time was not an issue. Keeping water out was.

The Light simply began to be there ahead of me. Moving toward it, gently, surely, it seemed the source of all that is good. I felt my soul smiling as I came nearer. Bliss.

A churning darkness, very unwelcome, began to pull me back, away from the glowing light. My being clamped in a cry of "NO!" but I was powerless. The lovely light receded as into a tunnel, as I was tugged away in a cold, dank nothingness.

As I became aware of sand in my face, pressure at my back, and feet and voices all around, I took in a hurting gasp of air. My husband Dick, who I later learned had almost died getting my leaden body off the bottom of the river, was making sure there was no water in my lungs in a most painful manner. There wasn't.

My son had asked, "Where is Mom?" When told I was joking about not being able to swim, he had screamed, "She CAN'T! DA-AD!" Dick was clowning in the water with a big cigar in his mouth, and made the first dive still gritting it in his teeth. When he came up, spit it out, gulped air and went down again, friends joined in the search.

It seems I was rolling in a ball along the current-driven bottom, far from my entry-point. Discovery was slow in the murky water, then recovery was in stages since rescuers had to keep surfacing for air. My body was so heavy that it took great effort to lift, not to mention my unwillingness to be rescued. I was no help.

My life at that point was a drifting sort of thing. Cub Scout Den Mother and PTA officer were behind me. I helped out at my husband's Orthotic and Prosthetic business only during vacations or sick leave for office staff. Entertaining friends, family, myself, of course... homemaking (not much-valued), that's all there was.

I felt sullen for a while after the 'incident', sulky, not at all my usual bubbly self. My husband was bewildered since it seemed obvious to him that I was blaming him for not letting me go. My friends soon tacitly avoided the subject, since I wasn't talking.

I felt no need to do any deep thinking. All my religious and philosophical searchings in the past had convinced me not to ask 'why' of anything. The one thing I was sure of—death—was not frightening. There were no suicidal urges; in fact life seemed to have gained a bit in value: colors brighter, birdsongs louder, life renewing around me, awareness of so much that had been taken for granted—all seemed to be pointing me in a direction.

Returning to the nursing field I had left to get married became a solid goal. If it was the idea of doing something useful with this life I still had, I don't recall. It's what I did.

That was in 1966. Nearly thirty years have passed, and what stands out are the many memories of people I've been with at their moment of death. An amazing assurance comes over me each time, and I feel I'm often able to communicate that Love-filled feeling of calm anticipation, of more Love ahead, to those moving on.

*Lonnie McDougle*

# The Living Christ

*Quincia Clay, a 58 year-old widow, mother of three living children, resides in Houston, Texas. She owns her own business, an art gallery, which also sells collectible figurines and other items. Her business has grown through repeat business, referrals and word of mouth because of her sincerity in offering each customer individually creative and money-saving ideas. She relishes most her children and grandchildren and thanks God daily for allowing her to watch them grow into beautiful young adults. She authored two books of poetry, "From the Heart of a Black Widow" and "Dove in the Window." Currently, she is writing a novel.*

It was a beautiful August 3 afternoon, quiet and peaceful. I had gone over to visit my fiancé across town. After dinner, we watched television awhile. "I'd better go," I told him about ten o'clock. "It sounds like a storm is coming up." I got up, put my sweater on and proceeded outside.

"It does look like rain. Maybe you'd better wait awhile."

"Oh, I'll be home in less than twenty minutes. I don't want the children frightened if a storm does come and I'm not home." The three oldest children were teenagers, the baby almost nine but their dad had died in his sleep just a few years earlier and the whole family had become very close and conscious of each others whereabouts. My fiancé lived about two miles from the downtown area and the trip home was mostly via freeway travel. I had just gotten onto the freeway when the rain began to pour down, blinding my vision, but I knew the area well and at that particular point there was not traffic except for a few cars a distance ahead, so I wasn't afraid.

Just as I was about to round a curve, my car suddenly lost control. It was as if the steering wheel was inoperable as the car hydroplaned, again and again, across and circled in the middle of the freeway. I could hear cars banging, not realizing it was my car hitting a parked car that had been abandoned on the freeway, evidently to be repaired later. I remembered lying down in my seat. I thought in fear of a whiplash, when I realized I was in mid-air looking down through the car seeing myself lying on the seat. Then I realized that I was me but without a body. I looked with my eyes or where my eyes would have been in my human body and could see for miles in every direction, way past city limits. The air was the freshest I had ever smelled, in my whole life. Then, the realization hit me that I must be dead. "This is beautiful" I remember thinking. "Absolutely beautiful." There was no pain at all, just a sense of total peace and contentment. Then my life began to roll in front of me as though I was seeing my life on a heavenly panoramic movie screen. I saw myself crawling as an infant less than a year old, then as a toddler and on and on, past the birth of my children, the loss of my husband, on to the present moment when the accident occurred. Then I saw my fiancé's grief on his face after he'd been told about my accident. I saw my Mom's grief also, literally saw it, when she was told that I had been killed but nothing compared to the peace that I felt. Until I saw the pain and felt it of my four babies sitting at a dinette table after they had been told, by a neighbor, that now they were motherless too. I could actually see their pain. I remember mouthing, "NO! NO! NO!" The next thing I remember was trying to sit up in my physical body in the car. I was still saying "no, no" when I raised up to find a wrecker man banging on the door. In fact, there were several wreckermen banging and begging to haul my wrecked car away. I remember feeling angered that here I had experienced the most unusual incident of my whole life, and all these people were concerned about was the almighty dollar that they could possible make off of the accident.

The back seat of the car had been thrown in the front seat, the drivers door was pressed in my side and the back of the car was crushed up to the back door but the front of the car had not been damaged at all. I didn't get a scratch except for glass shavings.

Before that incident, I had a terrible fear of death. I had a dreadful feeling of it being painful, frightening and ugly. But it was absolutely the most beautiful experience of my life with the exception of another, which I will explain later. And it changed my life completely. For one, it taught me without a shadow of doubt that there was more to the word 'life' than I had been knowledgeable of. I learned that the spirit lives on, though the physical body is lost through illness, accidents or however. I also learned that there was 'no sting' in death, that it is just a matter of 'crossing over.' Before the accident, I had become very materialistic and futuristic. But not once did the thought of anything materialistic cross my mind, there was no baggage being brought with me. I learned the power of love, realizing the intensity of peace and comfort like I'd never experienced before but after seeing my children's pain, there was instantly no question of giving that dynamic joy up for them. Also realizing that we have a destined 'time' and that night was not mine as it has been 24 years ago. But I remember it like yesterday. I also realized after seeing my life on that screen that evidently I had a very special purpose for even being here and that I especially wanted to fulfill that purpose. I feel that purpose is to share because the more I do share the more I'm given to share. I've also sensed a deeper contentment for what I already have rather than the materialistic drive, yet ironically, I've received more since my spiritual experience, in every area of my life, than ever before when striving so hard for it. I also learned, "that no man knoweth the day or the hour," as that car wreck happened so suddenly and unexpectantly and could very well have been fatal.

An Epiphany

About ten years after the near death experience, my life had changed so much. I began to seek knowledge on the spirit and soul. Among my reference materials was the Bible. I had been a regular every Sunday morning churchgoer, in the habit of <u>listening</u> to a good sermon but the ritual was more emotional than spiritual. But since I had already experienced a very personal encounter that *nobody anywhere* could *ever,* in this lifetime, take away from me, I wanted to learn more, know more than what I did know. Church became a more serious matter. I began to take my Bible with me.

I had to buy one to take because the one I had previously was on the livingroom table for show and emergency, in case I needed to look up a scripture for whatever reason. But my new

Bible was personal. When the minister would give his text scriptures, I would look them up and silently read with him, go home and read more of the scriptures. Soon, the Word got good to me and I fell in love with the author. Like all my prior idols, I wanted to know more and more about Jesus. The more I learned, the more I wanted to know. Then the desire to visit the *Holy Lands* became overwhelming. It was a place I had to go. The opportunity came when my church, The Evangelistic Temple, offered a 15-day tour. I had to go, nothing would stop me. The children were all grown-up, I had some vacation time available, the trip was on. There are no words to really describe the *Holy Lands*. Words like sacred, antiquated, ancient, holy, memorable, different, beautiful are just words—not even touching the surface of what the *Holy Lands* are like. You cannot describe the *Holy Lands,* you feel the *Holy Lands* through an awareness that you are really there, you feel the sun, the breeze, the tears as you soak in the sacredness and the beauty of Biblical land. And despite the long trip and many inconveniences that we take so for granted in America, such as water and bubble baths, there is such an appreciation that you made it there. Almost a taste of making it to heaven, at least for me. The trip was well planned with its scheduled tours and things to do. But <u>one</u> Wednesday was set aside to do whatever we wanted to do, individually.

We had been to Calvary the day before but there had been so many people there from all over the United States. Hundreds and hundreds of them separated in their own tour group. I wanted to go back to the "Garden" alone, to soak in the beauty I had felt in spite of the crowd the day before. So I did, very early the next morning and very much alone. There were only about a half dozen people around when I arrived. I sat in the "Garden" for awhile, marked the scriptures in my Bible and dated them. Scriptures about how Jesus' body had laid in a tomb, overwhelmed that I was setting right in front of that tomb and looking at the "Skull Hill" that the Bible writers had recorded. After awhile, I felt I had go to inside. Slowly, very slowly, I walked to the opening of the cave and looked in. It was empty. I could feel a power that began to engulf me as I stepped gently inside. There was a concrete bench nearby. I sat down as I realized my legs were trembling but not from fear. It was an awesome sense of love. I knelt my head to pray, when for the second time in my life, I saw my life roll in front of me, this time from in my mother's womb. I saw my mother fighting for her own life trying to birth me. I had not known this but later my mother confirmed it, saying it took almost three days of labor to get me here. I was shocked. But this time, I saw Jesus was there. And through all of the adversities in my life, He had been there. I saw the cotton patch days that I worked so hard in, the childhood loneliness, the birth of my children, the near-death of my last baby through sickle cell trait aggravations, the death of my husband, the car accident, the death of my son, my whole life was shown to me again, except this time I saw that I had never been alone, Jesus had been right there with me. Then I looked up sensing a presence and through my blinding tears, I saw Him with His hands on my shoulders. I cried so hard that morning, deep heartfelt tears. Someone not knowing would have thought I had just left a funeral. They could not have known, they were tears of awareness and gratitude. My life changed and is changing daily, growing deeper in knowledge and hopefully wiser but ever so humble.

*Now, I know, He was there all the time.*
*Now, I know, He will be there all the time.*
*Now, I know, He is alive.*
*Now, I know, I'm alive because of Him.*

*Qiuncia Clay*

# $\mathcal{S}$how Them the Way

*Chris Carson continued as a social worker for several years, then as a writer for training programs.*

In November, 1975, I lived in an isolated community between Houston and Galveston called Bayou Vista, near Hitchcock. The streets were divided by a ditch, one row of houses on the canal side, the street, a ditch, a street, row of houses, canal and so on. Thus communication with neighbors was difficult and most didn't want to talk to anyone, anyway.

I worked as a children's protective service caseworker in Galveston. I had recently assisted one of my associates with a case investigation on a missing family—the infant had been brought to the hospital brutally abused and dead.

My father and I argued over money—his mostly. I needed help and he didn't want to give it.

A close female friend had just cheated an acquaintance of mine out of a significant amount of money. I was using a lot of drugs and alcohol. I was grappling with my past, my present and my future. At 26, my body hurt from the abuse of alcohol. I hurt emotionally as I grappled with the effects of my judgment on other lives in my work and on my coming out, as I fought to resist the overwhelming realization that I was gay and did not have a clue what to do about personal acceptance.

I was depressed—mentally, physically and spiritually—when an acquaintance called for me to go to the bank with him on my day off. I agreed, dressed and went into Hitchcock with him at 8:00 am to the bank. He completed his business and asked if I'd like a screwdriver. We stopped at a neighbor's house for "brunch" drinks. The old man and his wife, dysfunctional, isolated and lonely, had a half-gallon of vodka, a lot of time and cartons of cigarettes. They invited me to drink, so I did. At lunch, we left for Joe's house. We ate a sandwich while he criticized another friend's behavior, then offered more drinks and later a gallon jar of "white crosses" or "speed." I simply—and thoughtlessly—took four. By now, it was late afternoon and we decided to do something for the night— like go to Houston. He called a mutual friend in town and made reservations at 1520 AD, a theme restaurant, for 8:00 pm.

We took an ice chest with ice, 12 ounce red plastic glasses, a half-gallon of this scotch (which I really didn't like) and a gallon of distilled water, drinking aggressively on the way. We drove to Mary's apartment in Houston. She was a semi-unemployed accountant with a crazed ex-husband, an alcoholic father and an obviously difficult future, but we were friends and I appreciated her acceptance, friendship and love.

We left for dinner. The restaurant was nice and expensive. They staged a Shakespearean-style performance while the patrons ate. We ordered steaks and were required in audience participation to go on stage in a sort of Conga Line to say or do something to the actors in stocks on stage. When I returned to the table, I remember collecting much silverware and putting them in my coatpocket. Joe and Mary emptied my coat of its new-found possessions but I became very nauseated when the meal arrived. They escorted me to the car to lie down and returned, worried, to finish the meal.

I lay there for awhile, uncomfortably, in the car. Then I sat up, wide awake, and impulsively drove off. For some reason, I decided to go to Winnie, Texas, to see a college classmate, a beautiful woman who had spoken to me very little in school and who was currently married to a serviceman still in Vietnam. Since it was late by now, and this would have been an entirely unexpected and unprecedented visit, I don't know what I could have been thinking about, but off I went happily, stranding my friends behind.

A few miles down the road I began to think about my situation, how silly it was to go to Winnie to see someone who had no knowledge of me at all, about my relationship with my father, with being gay, being worth more dead than alive with my insurance, and so on. I remember crying, sobbing in grief as this horrible dark feeling of absolute worthlessness came over me—a feeling that I had never before and have not since felt.

I decided to die. Through my tears I saw where a lane merged ahead on the left and the road was about six lanes across so I aimed for the dividing wall six lanes across at an angle and sped up as fast as I could go.

When I hit the wall, my head hit the top of the steering wheel and I felt the wheel split in two as I thought "Oh, shit! I'm dead!" Then darkness.

I remember vividly the looking up and seeing some number above a door, although my glasses had been lost and I am very near-sighted. Twenty years ago, I could have told you the number but now it is lost to me. I looked down on my body next and then I remember being in a dark tunnel moving along somehow. I was not in pain or discomfort. I do not remember any details in the darkness but the light was visible and growing.

Then I was surrounded by light, so intense I could feel it. I could not look, it just sort of permeated me. I felt this enormous love and well-being—peace—if you will. I had some sense of omniscience, or knowing everything. I felt that everything was right—as it should be. There was a purpose to everything. I felt knowledge and glimpsed godhood, I guess. There was absolute understanding, absolute love, absolute peace. Next I turned away and communication began with what others call a gate-keeper or angel or Jesus but it was someone. If I ever knew, I cannot remember now.

I heard that God depended on us to work on Earth. Intervention was not an option, somehow. I remember an explanation of Hell and Purgatory, though I am not Catholic or previously concerned with Purgatory. Once I had written a story in eighth grade about the guard at the crossing of the River Styx. I heard that really there is no purgatory and no hell. People who leave too soon or hurt others may (must?) watch what effect their actions have on others. Time is so different there. Watching the results can be painful, I understood, but I did not understand it to be mandatory. I just understood it- no heaven or hell. The good ones get to watch, too.

I learned that plans existed for me and that I had altered those plans by suicide. I could (or must?) go back. There was much to do. I remember not exactly wanting to leave but not resisting, either. Having seen the other side, I complied agreeably somehow and was imparted with these last words: "Show them the way."

I remember somehow telling my heart to start beating, we had work to do, and I woke up in a bright light with medical people cutting on me and wiring my jaws. I remember them asking if it hurt and I said yes. They told me they couldn't use an anesthetic because I had been in shock and could not feel the pain of oral surgery then. I believe they asked me if I wanted relief now. I felt the pain but in a new and different way—I said no and I was glad to have the pain somehow but it was only a ghost of other pain I have felt. Later they moved me to a bed and strapped me into some sort of traction. I had fractured my jaw, suffered a concussion, fractured ribs and dislocated my hip for many hours. My face looked like a Frankenstein, split between the lip and chin all the way to both ears, cuts and wounds all over. But I was at peace.

They gave me demerol for pain. My hip really hurt. A Methodist minister came to me in the room and spoke down to me. I was offended. I had just had the most powerful experience of my life and he was telling me some bull. I told him I was an atheist—leave me alone, and he did.

I went home to my parents during recovery. I drank bloody marys and malted milks through my wired jaws. When I got better and returned to work, I returned to my old ways. I quit the job and took a bicentennial tour of America. I remember at the Washington National Cemetery, as I walked by a huge oak tree in the Confederate section, I heard wailing and screaming and sadness of great depth, though there was no one around me. I remember crying in the hot noontime sun while walking to JFK's eternal flame. There, too, I was moved emotionally in rare depth. I felt the presence of many souls.

In 1983, I sold in-home products nightly. I lived with a relative I loved dearly and we both drank. I remember worrying as she suffered more and more. One Thursday night in July of 1983, I ran my appointment with a couple isolated in the woods. They bought my goods but insisted I eat with them. They questioned me and found my troubled concerns. They said they would pray for my relative. Friday night I caroused, Saturday I worked all day. I remember coming home to a smoke-filled house. My relative was carrying chicken frying in the skillet while an old school friend of hers ran screaming from the house that she couldn't take the craziness anymore. I could not communicate with my relative and left. I stayed at the Chief Motel on Main Street where I bought a big bottle of red wine and lots of cigarettes and watched television all night by myself. I went home Sunday night. My relative was asleep. I slept rock-solid and left early the next day to work. That afternoon four days or so after the strangers prayed, my relative admitted herself to the hospital. I was overjoyed that night that she was getting help, so glad I fixed myself a bloody mary and then another and another.

One month later, I slept through a small hurricane in Houston. It came through that night and I was sleeping drunk—missed the whole thing. In Family Week the next week, therapists convinced me that I needed to go to AA, too, so I did. I attended my first AA meeting at a gay chapter where I have been going ever since. That was 1983.

Since that time I have had a feeling that someone was with me, always. I have only once or twice felt briefly left alone. I started a business, my own, and struggled. I remember a year after a powerful relationship with a lover broke up that I was lonely. I remember praying to God for something specific. One of the steps in AA states that we pray to our higher power only for knowledge of his will for us and the power to carry that out. That night I prayed for someone to love, someone who could love me, too. The next week I met a man with eyes that shone. I knew he was the one. We have been together since. I cannot tell you how much he has meant to me, to my recovery, to my success, to my future. He has understood me at my worst and stood beside me in acceptance. He does not know the spiritual feelings I have but he accepts them as true for me. He is my gift from God and I have done as well by him as I am able.

My old drinking friends are all dead except one and she has one more year of sobriety than I do. What is it like now for me? My physical scars are almost all gone. I have my own business. I am a member of the community, active in civic affairs through a service organization. I own a house and beachhouse, trade the commodity markets, travel and read, love and live. I ache in strange spots as I age. I am always aware that my pains are my doing. My father died loving me and I loved him. We were friends, if not always in agreement. My Mother died a year later in my arms, peacefully, surrounded by her grown children and little grandchildren. My friends died loving me and I them. I have made new friends and my lover grows more important to me daily. I know now what I glimpsed so many years ago and I have it here with me. May you have it, too.

*Chris Carson*

# On The Valley Of The Shadow Of

*Nancy Noret Moore is currently enjoying traveling, teaching, learning and networking with peoples from many lands. She promotes individuals and organizations who are wanting to make the world a better place. She may be assisting a dying friend, helping a woman give birth, cooking fry bread at the Sundance in South Dakota, traveling to Geneva to support a spiritual elder at the U.N. Indigenous Peoples Conference, making a friend of a young girl in the Amazon Jungle who is apprentice to a tribal medicine man, or serving on a city council board in her local community. She continues to be involved in the movie theatre business with her family in Texas.*

> *There is a curious paradox that no one can explain.*
> *Who understands the secret of the reaping of the grain*
> *Who understands why spring is born of winter's laboring pain*
> *Or why we all must die a bit before we grow again.*

"You may not make it out of this alive!" were the words of a psychic friend who was getting "nudged and prodded" to speak to me about what she was seeing in her mind's eye. I was stunned and shocked! The possibility of me being involved in an automobile accident sent chills up my spine. She said, "You've just crossed a bridge; your vision seems to be blocked due to construction; there's an accident in progress; you may not have time to react; you seem to be driving something low to the ground. Maybe you can drive slower; maybe I'm being led to tell you this now so you can change something; nothing is written in stone, you know!" My mind raced; my heart screamed "No!" Why me? Why now? What was I to do with this information? Was I going to die? Was this to be taken seriously or taken as a joke?

I couldn't get it out of my mind. I prayed. I bargained with God and attempted to deny it all. I felt anger, ambivalence and deep sorrow. I went to church and I went to therapy. My emotions were going from one extreme to the next. Days and weeks and months passed with this gnawing pain. Finally, I simply surrendered. My prayer went something like this: "Dear God, please, if this can be taken from me, take it. If this is Thy will, I pray only for Thy highest and most magnificent will to be done." I gave up, and I went on with my life and felt a welcomed peace return to my heart.

Soon I was busy organizing a campaign in my community for a state senate race and the primaries were heating up. It was a bright spring day and I was heading to Austin for a strategy meeting. I picked up my five year-old son from school at noon and we traveled northward on Interstate 35. We had just crossed the Blanco River bridge and there in front of us, in our lane, was a huge flying object: a pickup truck upside down and flying. It hit us head-on. Time as I knew it slowed to a halt. I heard myself say, "It's happened; it's over." I deeply relaxed.

The world was different now. I was ascending above the car and countryside with gentle grace. Low hanging clouds and rays of light from a golden sun filled the blue sky. The Golden Gate opened around and seemed to be welcoming me. It was as though everything cleared up in the moments after the impact. There was a crispness and brilliance and clarity of everything I was seeing, hearing and feeling. I was in a place of knowing and was amazed at the beauty that pierced my total perceptions around me. I thought: "Wow!" I've certainly been in a fog." I looked down at the earth and saw a beautiful landscape with brilliant colors that vibrated a resonating softness. There was a tiny silver thread suspended on a breath of air connecting all of life together: the tree to the pond, the pond to the rock, the rock to the ants, the ants to the clouds—a world without end.

I was aware of a presence to the right of me and aware that "I" was ascending through, being washed by, and part of, something so wonderful. I asked the presence or Spirit what I was "in" and I heard, "You can call it an Ocean of Love." I felt awakened and in awe. I was experiencing how love was and is <u>always</u> present; how it is love that surrounds a nucleus inside a cell and it is what makes up the space around each cell. Love is what fills the space between two notes played on the piano, and it is the note itself vibrating to the constancy of truth. There is nothing that can separate us from Love. How could I have forgotten this?

I was remembering and embracing the truth that passes all understanding, the Truth that takes us Home.

I continued ascending high above the earth, being washed in the Ocean of Love. The earth herself was resonating to a vibration of sound. Then the sound seemed to fill me, as I too, was in that Oneness. Each sphere of the heavens seemed to play its own sound; its unique vibrational constancy, creating the harmonic music of the spheres. I was astounded to see such beauty and hear such perfection of peace.

The Spirit eventually spoke in words to me, gently asking, "Are you indeed complete?" I remember answering without hesitation that I wasn't through with my life, that I still had a lot of work to do. Spirit answered, "We want you to breathe now. That's good—breathe deeply. We are with you always and remember: everything will be okay!" It was as if a slight adjustment in the lens of my eyes was made and I switched to this earthly dimension.

I was now physically lying in a ditch, people and cars all around me. A woman sat beside me, a woman I did not know. She was holding my hand and touching my heart. She told me that I had been in an accident, that a truck had hit our car head-on, and that my son Jason was ready to go in an ambulance to the hospital. I could hear him crying at some distance away from me. He was scared. I went to him in "spirit" and told him that he would be fine now, that he could stop crying. He did. I spoke again to the woman beside me and told her how guilty I felt because my son was hurt. As soon as I "thought guilty," the energy of unconditional love left. This "guilt energy" started filling my body. This was the first negative energy to enter me after being purified and cleansed by the Ocean of Love. It entered my right leg, quickly running through my body to manifest excruciating pain in the very injured or crushed part of me. It hurt! I quickly said to the woman, "I am going to think about this guilt tomorrow." As soon as I chose, the negative energy left my body and I could see it going back to the Light. This gentle woman was my advocate and liaison. The police asked her questions and she in turn asked me: "They want to know if you have a doctor in San Marcos." I (the little I) said "No, I don't ever go to the doctor." Then I heard Spirit tell me the names of two doctors. I said, "Dr. Primer and Dr. Nemeth, please." The police radioed in; both doctors were waiting for us when we arrived at the hospital. They were the specialists that my son and I needed to treat our injuries.

Before I was taken to the hospital, Spirit insisted that I ask this woman her name. I said, "Excuse me, but what is your name?" She smiled and said, "Why, my name is Valle." I said, "'Valley!'—as in peaks and valleys, or 'Yea, though I walk through the Valley of?'" She chuckled and said, "Well, yes, I suppose you could think of it that way." I laughed when I heard Spirit's laughter at how funny life is.

Valle rode with me to the hospital that day. I overheard her to say to her husband, "I'm going with this lady. Please turn around and pick me up at the hospital."

Valle and her husband had been visiting relatives in South Texas and were on their way to Oklahoma. Due to the wreck, they were caught in a miles-long traffic jam that had to be rerouted via the frontage road. She got out of their stopped car, told her husband, I've got to go help someone." And she walked through the line of cars and trucks to me. She said later that she had never done that before or since. Valle was a teacher's aide for Spirit that day.

I walked through "the valley" for days and weeks afterwards. The veil between the worlds was incredibly thin. With only a slight adjustment of my intent, I could travel from one to the other. I learned—There is Here, as Above, so Below. Love surrounded me in Spirit and love surrounds me here in this dimension. The only thing different is that here on earth we collectively are invested in the belief that we are separate from our Home of God's unconditional love, and we are in great pain because of that belief. In our lives we create many dramas as a result, and that perpetuates our fears. My work began that day and continues to this day. A commitment to love brought with it a response of constant vigilance to what I choose in every moment. Is it love or is it fear? Being in pain told me I was forgetting.

When I was with Spirit in "the Remembering," the healing process was truly joyous. What I call miracles were happening daily. My son was looking through the hospital room's Bible at the pictures and said, "Mom, Mom, this is what was floating all around our car!" I looked and saw his little finger pointing to a picture of beautiful angels. Tears filled my eyes.

We had a most extraordinary physical therapist who agreed to participate on all levels of healing with Spirit. When it came time for therapy, I would have to wait for my body to be filled by Spirit with love energy and then I could move broken bones without fear or pain. I could actually feel the energy enter through the bottom of my feet and the top of my head. Every morning I looked forward to this experience—to be with this earthly angel and Spirit. I found it strange that I could not remember her name. She would remind me each day and still I forgot. I asked Spirit what was going on here. Spirit said, "You know her by another name." So, I asked her if she had a middle name or maybe a nickname. She said, "Yes, it's Joy." Once again, the laughter! I have never forgotten that "Joy cometh in the morning."

One of the last times Spirit lifted me from my body came as the sun was rising on a Sunday. I could see from my hospital window the glow of the city as light covered it with a golden hue. I gasped as I saw the gold of the Golden Gate again. The power of Love flooded my room and it felt overwhelming. I started to shield myself from it. Catching myself in mid-defense, I decided to open my heart and let in this wondrously powerful sight. I took a deep breath and shut my body's eyes, and in that same moment I opened my inner eyes to Spirit. This time I was riding on the wing of an incredibly large bird. I could see the top of her head and the left wing as I nestled on her shoulder. I watched as the long stride of her wing gracefully stretched downward toward the earth. The earth below was speeding past us. This was a flight into my future life. The bird took me to many distant lands and I met people in Spirit that later I would actually meet in life. I got glimpses of the places I would travel and the work I would be doing. The last place we visited was Egypt where I was flown through a healing ceremony of colors. Again, I was bathed cellularly, this time with pure colors: royal blue, gold, green, magenta and on and on we flew. When she gently left me that day in my hospital room, I knew it would be the last time for awhile. It felt good to be alive. I heard Spirit's gentle words; "In all your peaks and valleys, remember the joys and laughter. Be gentle with yourself. Be who you are. We are with you always."

*Nancy Noret Moore*

# Prodigal Son Returns Home More Than Once

*"I worked 24 years at a chemical plant in Houston as a craft foreman. I got tired of my job in 1994 and the new concern was tired of me so I opened a small car lot in Porter, Texas. I sell work cars to working people. This new business has been fun. My daughter and I run it. Business has been good but money alone won't save me. I have to do the next right thing."*

Maybe the answer is in the Old Testament. The Jews watched the Red Sea part and their lives were spared. A little later they whipped out a gold calf and worshipped it. I've heard preachers ask, "How could they?" Easy for me to understand— I did the same thing. I don't believe that people who have had this kind of experience are special. I just believe that most of us are hardheads who have to be shown. After saying my life didn't change, I have to say there's never been a day in forty years that I haven't thought of the light.

The ends of my toes got numb first, then my feet and legs. Before it was over, I was in the hospital dying. Doctors never found out what it was. They thought I might have picked up a tick off a rabid bat in one of the caves I had explored, around Austin.

I'm getting ahead of myself. I was born and raised in Austin, Texas. I was fifteen years old when this paralysis hit me. I was raised in a church but I had cast that aside for a more adventuresome life. I was self-willed and going wild. Couldn't stand school then. Forty years later I still get a sick feeling when I hear a bell ring. I couldn't do as I was told. It was more fun to do what I wanted.

In and out of (juvenile) jail didn't seem to slow me down drinking and dancing. Now, when this paralysis hit me and they put me in the hospital, I didn't worry much about it cause I thought I'd live forever. Well, I'd been in the hospital about ten days with the numbness creeping up my body. When it got around my heart, I started getting worried. The sheet was jumping off my body. My heart was laboring to keep working. That night it dawned on me that I wasn't waking up in the morning. This wasn't a movie: I was out of here.

I had always thought I was as tough as an Indian warrior but I was frozen with fear. I started praying—not a light easy prayer you might pray over dinner but an abandoned, holding-nothing-back kind of prayer. I surrender, God! Then something happened. I started moving real fast, not my body but my mind. I was gone from that hospital bed, gone to another place. Rushing through space towards something. The something I was rushing toward was a light brighter than the sun. It was wonderful. I could feel it! But I was still the same person who had been in the hospital bed, so I was terrified. I didn't know where I was.

A voice from the light talked to me but it didn't seem happy. It said, "What do you think you've been doing?" It was like the voice of a man. I was still frozen with fear. I tried to explain my life but the voice knew everything.

Another voice came from the light, like a woman's voice. This voice took up for me. And these two voices talked about me to each other. I didn't know where I was. It wasn't like the male voice was mad at me, just disappointed. And the light took me in. And that was all that there ever was. Nothing more or after ever was so wonderful. Words cannot explain the feelings of love and joy: a river of love coming from forever! I felt like I knew where I was: I was home! As I write this forty years later, it still makes me cry.

Since then, I've watched doctors and scientists try to explain this on TV. Some say it is a lack of oxygen, triggering something in the brain. I've got news for them hard-working people. I don't believe they will ever get to look at that light in a test tube. But I can say with certainty that someday the light will look at them.

There was more, but it was blocked from my mind. I woke up the next morning and the light was still with me. I knew I would get well and I knew that I would turn my life around.

I got well. I learned to walk again in a few weeks. Thoughts changed but I didn't change my life like I had promised. I fell way short of what I thought my life should have been. By dinner the next day after my healing, I was back doing things my way. You might ask, "How could you go through that and not change?" I don't know. I didn't change my life. I tried and tried to forget it. I could put it from my mind sometimes—almost a day. I drank. I worked for a large company. I tried throwing myself in the corporate world worrying about company business, gambling, drinking more.

Maybe the answer is in the Old Testament. The Jews watched the Red Sea part and their lives were spared. A little later they whipped out a gold calf and worshipped it. I've heard preachers ask, "How could they?" Easy for me to understand— I did the same thing. I don't believe that people who have had this kind of experience are special. I just believe that most of us are hardheads who have to be shown. After saying my life didn't change, I have to say there's never been a day in forty years that I haven't thought of the light.

Looking back, I realize that I could've been a bank robber, but for the light.

I believe that this light can be reached through prayer. At fifty three years old, I joined a twelve-step group and began to change my life. I became willing to listen to directions. It became reasonable for me to believe that I didn't know nothing. If I wanted to walk the high road, I had to ask a power higher than myself to walk me up the steps. And he did. Isn't it strange that some of us prodigal sons leave home more than once?

I pray that you have good in your life. The light is your good.

*Jack Nicholson*

Look Through the Eyes of God

*Glenn Brymer is 44 years old and retired from the U.S. Army (RA) in 1971. Since that time, he has worked as an automobile mechanic, control panel wireman, electrician, construction worker, metal smelter, salvage diver, geophysical seismographic technician (land & marine), convict, assistant editor, welder, sandblaster, spray painter, tree trimmer and lumberjack, lumber mill worker & entrepreneur. He has also been a nomadic wanderer & backpacker. He is currently residing in Houston planning his future priorities.*

On March 3, 1971, at 010:35 in the morning, an incident occurred on a U.S. Army surface-to-air missile site in West Germany on the former Czechoslovakian border. The missile site was the "A" Battery designated "Alpha Forward" of the 3rd Battalion of the 7th Artillery of the 32nd Air Defense Command. I had been assigned to this unit as a power generation specialist in November of 1969; I was 17 years old. This missile site was operational and involved in on-going Air Defense operations against Soviet and Czech aircraft, helicopters and jets that were flying out of air bases just inside the Czechoslovakian border.

In the center of the missile site stood a steel tower with a siren on top. Whenever the radar operators in the fire control center detected enemy aircraft flying and closing on or crossing the border, they would hit the siren and it would split the air with its wailing. This was the call to action; when it went off, it jolted everyone on the site into motion! It would have taken a jet flying over one thousand miles per hour only a *very* short time to reach our site which was seventy-five plus miles from the border. We could possibly become a smoking crater in ten to fifteen minutes or less. This was for real! This happened; in fact, it happened a lot! Sometimes that siren would go off two or three times day and night. It really made your adrenalin pump. It was scary to think what was maybe coming in on us.

The main building where the crew ate, slept and lived was called the "ready room." They were always ready to go—just let the siren scream and away they would run. Sometimes we were given the Ready Alert orders. This meant that we were to have the entire battery (150 men approximately) called in, get on our combat gear and our weapons and prepare to go to war. We never really knew if it was for real or just a test. During these alerts, we could be given MOVE-OUT orders. We were expected, if it was called for, to pick up the entire missile site and become a mobile missile group able to go by land or by aircraft to wherever we were told to go. When we actually did move out, it was wild because we had to do it in one hour or less if we could and we could!

On March 1, 1971, a "Ready Alert" was given to our unit commanders. This was not one of the usual alerts. It was not from our Battalion commander or even from our top 32nd ADCOM Commander. This alert was put in force by the North Atlantic Treaty (NATO). They had apparently picked our missile site at random from the hundreds of other such sites to have an extended fiield test and evaluation by the NATO High Command. This was serious—they were serious. This was not like any evaluation we had ever had thrown at us in the past. This one was to go on for three days and two nights under bad weather conditions. The missile site was a sea of mud and snow and it was raining and snowing at times, very nasty conditions in which to conduct war games and attack scenarios for evaluation. We were given field "problems" ranging from ground attack by tanks and infantry, air attacks by jets, nuclear attacks, gas attacks, biological attacks, and different combinations of all these attacks. The evaluators threw problem after problem at us; they made it sometimes impossible to do yet we were still to do our "best." This went on hour after hour for three days and two nights. It was hard, both physically and mentally, and it even affected our emotions at times, too. It was really something! It was a make-believe war! Do you know how it feels to be "killed" when you are trying hard to accomplish an objective under combat conditions? It's very frustrating at times: I was "killed" five times in the course of those evaluations. It was nerve-wracking. This was a test, an evaluation; it was not real. It was crazy, but we gave it our best time after time after time. It wore us out and still the field "problems" kept happening one on top of another. We started to get a little wild in our efforts to handle them.

I was 19 years old. There were five men in the engineer section including myself. We were in charge of the 45 kilowatt generators and the gear that goes with them, all eight of them mounted on wheels and trailers. They were in concrete and brick stalls, two to a stall. One of the generators did not have a truck in front of it ready to hook up to it—that truck had broken down. So we used our truck to hook it for the move-out. When my partner first backed up, he rammed into the generator and trailer, pushing it into the back wall. I knew one of the men was back there, between the wall and the generator. The truck rolled forward as the driver put the clutch in. I jumped between the wall and the truck heading for the back of the shed to get to the man whom I thought was in serious trouble. As I got between the truck and the wall, I heard the motor on the truck rev up. Then I heard the clutch being let loose. The truck jumped backwards! I tried to get out from between the truck and the wall, but my combat web gear became hung on the back of the truck. My steel helmet, caught between the truck and the wall, was being crushed. I put my hand on the right side of the truck and pushed—my body moved far enough so that the helmet was jerked out from between the truck and the wall. It was under such so much tension that it popped off my head and flew through the air, making a sound like "Spooooong" as it came off! I was caught between the wall and the truck and crushed into the concrete and double-brick wall twice before going partway through the wall the third time. The driver gained control of the truck and pulled forward (I learned later that his foot had slipped off the clutch due to the mud that was on it after he had revved up the motor to keep it from dying). The first time the truck hit me and drove into the wall, there was a flash of pain that shot through my body and I thought, "I've broken my arm!" The second time it hit me, I knew that my arm was broken because I could feel it and hear it break! Well, the third time the truck drove me into the wall (which started to come apart as I went into it), I thought "Son-of-a-bitch! Enough already!" The driver gained control and pulled the truck forward about ten yards, dragging me along, still hung by my combat equipment harness. I jerked myself off the back of the truck.

I looked at the truck, at the generator shed wall and at my left arm. My left hand was lying on top of my boot! I thought, "Oh, shit!" I swayed backwards a step and my arm swung around to the right side of my body. As it did this, the whole sleeve just flattened against my chest as if there was nothing in it. I reached down and grabbed my arm and pulled it up against my stomach. My left arm was partially amputated at the shoulder. It was almost completely torn off! I could feel the blood running down my side under all my clothing and gear. I thought it felt like warm chocolate syrup had been poured inside my shirt.

The next ten minutes were very intense ones. I could see something above me—sort of—and looked at it. It appeared to me to be some type of cloud made up of hundreds of small black and white checkers. It shimmered and buzzed as it started to sweep over the top of me. I wondered what it was and then it came to me that if this cloud covered my vision, it would kill me. I didn't know what it was, then it hit me. This must be what shock looked like. I was going into shock! For a moment I was stunned, then my training took over and I took action.

A very strange thing happened then. It was as if I turned and went inside myself, as if I was taking an inventory of what was going on inside me. I saw my heart beating really fast, too fast. My breathing was very rapid and a lot of blood was leaving my body. I willed my heart to slow down, then I slowed my breathing and I tried to slow the blood going to my arm. After I had done all this, I turned outward. It was strange. I suddenly was outside my body again. It struck me then that I had seen the inside of myself looking at an anatomy book. The cloud of checkers had stopped and was going back and fading. When it was gone, everything focused crystal clear and everything became very sharp. It was pretty weird. I then stumbled over to the side of the road and down by the side of it a few feet in the blast-depression area.

By this time, the driver had stopped the truck and gotten out to see what had happened. The man I thought had been behind the generator and trailer came running up yelling "You killed him!" The driver started to walk in circles like he was freaking out or something. I found out later that he had a breakdown and had to be taken to the hospital. One of my buddies was beside me and helped me lie down on the ground. By now, it felt like there was a lot of blood because I was soaking wet inside my gear. My buddy was screaming for the medic. The sergeant held my head; the medical corpsman worked on me to stop the blood and find out how badly I was hurt. As he was working on me, my platoon sergeant knelt beside me, holding my hand in his. I told him that I was scared and he told me it was OK and just relax. The look on his face comes back to me a lot, because it was like nothing I had ever seen before. He was a hard man to please and tough as hell, but at that moment he had the softest, kindest and most caring look on his face. As they put me into the jeep, my left arm fell to the floor! The medic told someone to pick up my arm and put it on my chest. I held onto it with my right hand. The medic turned around to look at me and he reached back and grabbed hold of the hood of my parka and jerked it back! Apparently a lot of the blood inside my clothes had drained into the hood. When the medic jerked it back, all of the blood spilled out and hit the floor of the jeep and splattered all over the medic and the specialist! I could feel myself getting weak.

I went through what is now called a "Near-Death Experience." This experience only lasted for a brief moment in time. But the aftereffects were to last for long afterwards. It was a very transcendental spiritual experience and it was very intense. I didn't want to die! I had had a hard life up till I joined the Army. Being a soldier and being in the military was the high point of my young life. I was just starting to really do good for a change and felt proud for the first time in my life. I didn't want to die! I was very frightened from the injuries I had suffered. I had stopped myself from going into deep shock; the medic had done all that he could do to stop the bleeding! I was only 19 years old. I got scared, real scared. WHAT WAS I GOING TO DO? WHAT COULD I DO?

That is when I thought about GOD, GOD, THIS WAS A GOD JOB! I'LL CALL ON GOD. I'LL ASK GOD TO SAVE ME YA!!!!!!!

This thought was in my mind and it was working overtime! I started to ask God for my life and to save me from death! Then

I stopped—did I really believe in God? I mean, did I REALLY believe? Well, yes and no. Yes, I thought that there was a greater power that was behind everything that went on in the universe. No, I didn't believe that the Bible was the whole truth of the matter. I believed that there was a source though that was behind everything that went on. I remembered back to when I was about 6 years old and one day looking out over a field of tall grass and trees surrounded by the city at sunset with the sun turning all into a golden shade that to me looked beautiful. At that moment I realized the scope, the vastness, the depth of the world and in that moment something happened inside me: a "knowing" sort of took place. I thought of the Indians that I had met, about their ceremonies and their beliefs. I thought about the Mormon religion in which I had just been baptized recently. I thought about all of this in that moment and I weighted it all and summed in up in my mind. YES I DID BELIEVE! so I started to ask that power that was the sum total of all people's religious beliefs and mine for help! I had it all in my mind, when once again I stopped and thought, WHO AM I TO ASK GOD'S HELP?

I thought, what have I done to deserve to be saved? I wasn't a saint, I didn't lead a real pure life. I had faults, I drank, I cussed, I had impure thoughts. I thought about all of this and looked at it. I might not be a saint but I had lot of good in me and I decided that since I REALLY needed help because I really didn't want to die, the only thing to do was let GOD make that decision. So in my mind, in all that was me at that moment, I got it all together. All my beliefs in a greater power, and all that was me and I spoke to the universe on a wide band to the far ends of everywhere. This is what I sent out: GOD, here I am and I'm in real trouble. I need your help. I am afraid that I'm dying and I'm very scared because I don't want to die, I need help. I don't know if I'm good enough to be saved though so I'm going to open up everything that is me and you look at what is in me and you make the call God because I don't know. YOU make that decision. It is in your hands your will be done! With that I surrendered and opened up and let it all go. I WAS ANSWERED IN THAT VERY INSTANT!!!! I had made the connection!!!

Everything disappeared! The missile site was gone, the jeep, medic and all else were just gone! The pain, the fear, all gone! I was somewhere else. It seemed like I was floating in a gray void. I was not really aware of my body but it seemed like it was just sort of floating there in that place. It was very silent there. I wondered what was happening, where was I? Then this feeling came to me—it seemed to spread through all of me. Mere words cannot describe it totally. Words like LOVE, UNCONDITIONAL LOVE, CARE, GREAT CARE, WARMTH, PEACE, SEREN-ITY—these words are what come to me to describe those feelings, that presence that was in me at that time in that place. I had never felt anything like it before. It was beautiful.

Then a voice spoke to me and it seemed to come right into my mind. It was a man's voice that seemed like he spoke to you the way a father or grandfather would speak to his child whom he loved very much and cared for greatly. This voice said: GLENN, YOU DO NOT DIE. I asked what he meant. GLENN, YOU DO NOT DIE. YOU CONTINUE. I said that I did not understand what he meant. I KNOW GLENN, THAT YOU DON'T UNDERSTAND. THIS WILL HELP YOU TO UNDERSTAND.

With that said, a point of light appeared in the void and it came towards me and as it came towards me in an arch, it grew larger and larger till it filled my vision till I thought I would fall into it as it came to me. It was beautiful! It was like a very white sun, dazzlingly luminous, shooting off streamers of light all around. It was immense before me. Then in the very center a black square opened up and images started flashing in it very rapidly. It was as if millions of pictures were being flashed before me. The images were being recorded by me but to try and say what they were is hard. I can only say that I was given a sense of seeing life going on and on in all its evolutions and cycles everywhere in creation. I was being shown that truly you in fact don't die—you continue. The "screen" closed and the "sun" went back the way it had come till it disappeared and I felt as if I was going backwards. The voice spoke again and it seemed as if he was going away from me fading in the distance as I was going backwards faster. He said to me as I was going NOW YOU KNOW, GLENN.

Then I was back on the missile site and on the stretcher in the jeep. There was no longer any pain or fear, I felt very calm and serene. I still didn't know if I was going to make it but it no longer frightened me. Everything was OK. It was very strange that feeling that was in me then. I felt at peace. I knew—I had been shown—all was OK. It was very strange the feeling that was in me then. I felt at peace. I knew—I had been shown—all was OK. Following these events, I was rushed to the local medical facility. Once there, all turned to chaos with nurses working and a doctor checking me. The doctor realized quickly that I needed better care than they could give me and called for a MedEvac by helicopter to the 33rd field hospital in Wurzburg. Some time went by before the chopper arrived but it soon came in and landed very fast. I was loaded onto the chopper and the pilot took off even quicker. (I later went back to thank the pilot and crew for helping me and found out that the pilot had served several tours of duty in Vietnam as a MedEvac pilot; that was why his landings and takeoffs were so fast, not like what you see on TV).

Upon landing at the 33rd Field Hospital, I was again surrounded by chaos as the medical people did their work. I was awake during all this but at one point I passed out because the next thing I knew, I was on an operating table with my left arm tied up in the air on a pole and two doctors were discussing whether or not to amputate the arm.

I looked at my arm and it really looked like something out of a butcher shop. I turned and said to the doctors to put my damn arm back on because I was from Texas and would need it later. The doctors were surprised and asked me if I was in any pain. I said no and you still had better put my arm back together or I'd come hunting them later. A mask was put over my face and the lights went out.

Upon waking up, I was disoriented but a male orderly standing next to me started talking to me and asked if I knew where I was and what had happened. It came to me quickly—I grabbed for my left arm. The orderly stopped me and said I still had my arm and showed me. It was on me OK: it looked like something out of a Frankenstein Movie with large and small stitches going all the way around my shoulder. It sure looked strange. I looked down at my left hand and tried to wiggle my fingers. By golly, they moved. The orderly asked me if I was in any pain. I realized that it did hurt like hell. He called for a nurse who gave me a shot of narcotic called *Demerol*. The orderly said good night to me. As I was wondering why he had said that, I went under due to the drug.

Weeks went by and several operations were done. They kept giving me shots of the same narcotic drug along with other drugs every three or four hours. I thought that the Demerol was some mighty fine stuff because it took away the pain and any thoughts, too, except for how good it made me feel. They lowered the drug dosage and moved me to another room with other patients. One evening, the lessening of drugs in my body allowed me to start my thought process up again. I went back through the whole thing. When I got to the plea for a higher power's help, it all came rushing back to me. I was stunned and shocked by the realization of what had happened to me. My thoughts split in two, one side going over the experience and the other going over what had I had learned nineteen years of my life. When I remembered my NDE and that the comparison with my life was very uneven and unequal, I didn't have the emotional strength to compare my lessons in life with what the NDE had shown me. The comparison between the LOVE, CARE and COMPASSION of the experience and my life were just too vastly different. It overwhelmed me and caused me to "freak out." It was very scary. It was like trying to put a square peg in a round hole. I tried to stop what was happening but it was out of my control. It kept going faster and faster, back and forth. I started to get very scared and got out of bed and went down to the nurses station for help. There were two Captain nurses on duty. One asked what was wrong. I started to say something but what came out was only gibberish. The imme- diately gave me a shot and put me to bed.

The next morning, they wheeled me down to the Psychiatric Unit. A Captain social worker listened to me tell about what hap- pened and that was all. It happened again several weeks later. Back to the social worker I went, still not getting any real help. Twenty years later, I sent for a copy of my army medical records. The social worker had said that I was having a situational mal- adjustment precipitated by my arm injury. He wrote the same thing about the second visit, noting that I should be seen by a psychiatrist in the United States. I was never ever talked to again by anyone concerning the problems I was having. I never got any help for the mental, emotional and spiritual problems I was dealing with, not from the doctors, not from the chaplains, not from my family, not from anyone except maybe a fellow vet or two.

My world had changed but I couldn't really tell just how much. Upon being airevac'ed back to the States, I was flown to Fort Sam Houston in San Antonio, Texas.

This was in June of 1971. The hospital was full of thousands of men who had been in Vietnam and now were recovering from their wounds. Some of them did not recover but died. I had gotten to know some of those who died; it hurt very much to see them die. It was a very crazy place to be during those days. So many of us had been hurt and were suffering both physically and mentally that it was like a living thing among us. We helped each other when possible; we were bound together by our wounds and our pain I grew very close to those guys who had been through the war. I got to know them very well. There was just so much hurt and pain, missing legs and arms, burns that made people look like melted wax! During this time, I was comparing my NDE with what was going on around me. It was like the difference between night and day. It was very radical. I could not understand what was happening because I did not have very much wisdom then. All I could do was to handle what was happening on a daily basis.

How does Love Compare to War? It doesn't! Well, a lot of what I was going through in daily life didn't compare, either. Try to understand how I was seeing things. Here I had this incredible experience dealing with something as awesome as the power of GOD and being exposed to that unconditional love, caring and compassion, and then going out and living in America in the early 1970's. It was very unsettling, to say the least. Most of the time, I was walking around in some sort of shock. At the hospital, another patient and I would sit and talk and talk. I heard and saw so much horror that I became numb. When I would think about my NDE and compare it with what I was seeing and hearing, it just totally HURT!!!! I COULD NOT UNDERSTAND WHAT WAS GOING ON AROUND ME!!! WHY WAS THIS HAPPENING!?!? There just seemed to be a lot of opposition in everyday living when I compared the feelings of the NDE brought out in me as compared to what I saw going on around me in the world. It caused me to feel very uncomfortable and to a large degree caused me to feel a lot of distress and pain— physically, mentally, emotionally and spiritually.

So what did I do? I did the one thing that I had learned that would take the pain away. I started drinking and taking drugs to escape. I later learned that this was just throwing gas on the fire and causing me even more problems. But I didn't know that then. This was the beginning of a very vicious cycle that would go on and on for many years to come. Between the problems of having a maimed left shoulder that was giving me constant pain, recurring flashbacks and intrusive thoughts from the missile sight and the aftereffects of the NDE, I found myself up a creek, so to speak, and at that time, I had no idea where the paddle was or that there was even a paddle! I was a mess but didn't understand any of it at all.

I turned to the Veterans Administration for help in 1972 but didn't get any help. Then again in 1985. Still no help, just more drugs. I thought it over and decided that the next time I talked to a doctor, I would tell him that I didn't care if they believed or not in a Higher Power or God or what, but to me it was real so please deal with it and don't just refuse to document it or talk to me about it. Then in 1987 I went into the V.A. hospital here in Houston and made a connection with a therapist who understood much of what I was going through. Her name was Elizabeth Szabo. She helped me greatly in understanding what had happened to me throughout my life and gave me many tools with which to work on my own.

Then I went to San Antonio, Texas, where I met a doctor at the Vet Center who helped me understand even more. He, too, was understanding and caring. While in San Antonio, I read a Sunday news magazine that had a story concerning a local Army nurse who was stationed at Fort Sam Houston. The story told all about her work and research into Near-Death Experiences. This was the first time I had really seen anything in print. What she had to say hit home with me. I went to Fort Sam to find her. For the first time, I connected with someone who really knew about NDE's. Dr. Corcoran met with me and asked me some questions, then showed me a tape of ten other people who had NDE's. The tape shocked me. I had no idea that there were others having the same problems that I was having. I no longer felt isolated. She also gave me a book called "Coming Back to Life" by P. M. H. Atwater.

I took the book home with me and read it throughout the night. As the sun came up, I finished it. With tears streaming down my face, in great joy I greeted the new day in its golden beauty. Ms. Atwater's book went into great detail about the aftereffects that show up in one's life after having an NDE. It was incredible how much of what had gone on with me from the star was explained by her. So many of the things that had gone on were shown to me clearly. I wasn't crazy, nor had I been imagining things. No other book had ever gone into such great detail concerning the aftereffects.

I went back to Dr. Diane Corcoran and told her about reading the book and the effect it had on me. She was very happy for me. I asked for Ms. Atwater's phone number and she gave it to me. I then called Ms. Atwater. She was on a speaking tour. But I did reach her and talked with her about her book and other things. I told her thank you, thank you, thank you for writing the book because it had helped me so very much. She, in turn, thanked me for calling her to thank her because at the time she was coming under much criticism because of her controversial research and statements and views concerning Near-Death Experiencers and what was happening around them and to them. I was the first experiencer to have contacted her after the book had come out and my talk with her helped her to deal with the problems she was having. We have remained friends since that time. She was brave enough to fly in the face of adversity and say things that no one else was saying about what was going on with the people who were having problems with life after going through an experience. Her book is a must for anyone, including friends and family of someone who has had an NDE. It has information in it that no other book has concerning aftereffects.

I have learned so much about NDE's and related subjects that I can now understand why I went through so much strife in my life. I know now that we are all learning and teaching lessons and that if there were new problems in our lives that life would be perfect and we would not have any lessons to learn. We would already be in Paradise. I am not as driven as I once was and I have much more wisdom now with which to temper my thoughts. I find now that I exist in a state of acceptance concerning events. I prefer solitude. But I still do my service in teaching and learning daily and helping others when I can. The future will reveal itself as it happens. This is reality. This is life. We are not just bodies. We have souls, too. There is a cosmic plan unfolding throughout everywhere and everyone and everything. The lessons are there for you to grow both the good ones and the bad ones. Welcome to your life. May you all be blessed. In closing, I wish to thank everyone who helped me recover the use of my left arm and those others who helped, too. A special thanks to Elizabeth Szabo, Diane Corcoran, Phyllis Atwater, Dr. Abney, Dr. Batte, my sister Patsy and many others who helped in their own way. Thank you. You are all special to me.

*Glenn P. Brymer*

# $\mathcal{R}$efused at Heaven's Gate

*Jerry L. Casebolt was born in Harrison Co. Hospital, Harrison, Ark., USA, in 1940 while his father was on U.S. Army rehabilitation. Six months later, he moved with his family to Colorado, where he grew up for the first 12 years of his life on or near farms and ranches. After a stay of 18 months in Kansas, his family moved to Lubbock, Texas. He graduated from Cooper Rural High School near Lubbock.*

*Jerry has expanded his awareness and abilities through extensive training and education from a very broad spectrum of courses and experiences over the years. His formal education includes a Bachelor of Science degree in Life Sciences and a degree in Chiropractic from Palmer College of Chiropractic where he graduated Magnum Cum Laude in 1978. Undergraduate work was done, mostly, at Texas Tech University.*

*He currently enjoys an eighteen years old practice in Liberty Hill, Texas. His practice includes specialties in Kinesiology, Craniopathy, Chiropractic sports medicine, and three years as a Chiropractor for women's track at the University of Texas, traveling with the team to major track events.*

*Pamela K. Casebolt is his wife, administrative director, best friend and capable boss. She has borne four children and shared 27 years of her life with him. They have been gifted with seven grandchildren.*

*Previous occupations have been: Systems Engineer, Data Processing Operations Manager, Electronics Technician, Electrician, Polaris Atomic Powered Submarine 7½ years, Missile Electronics, Computer troubleshooter, electrician, cowboy, farmer, construction worker, and numerous other occupations.*

*Jerry is a part-time writer, submitting occasional columns for the Liberty Hill Independent Newspaper, on health issues, health problems, and occasional political issues pertinent to his locale. While in the Navy, he won a Freedoms Foundation Award for an essay called "I am an American, enemy of Tyranny," and a poem called "American Farmer," He is currently writing a 5 book series which is a fiction whose 12 main characters have had death experiences and involves the very political foundations of America.*

*Other special awards were a Navy Commendation for Service, a clinical Proficiency Award, and a Texas Citizen of the Year Award. He has taught weekend seminars, and short workshops on Out-of-Body Experiences, Near-death Experiences, Alternative Healing Techniques with sound, light, and symbols, Touch for Health, Soul Travel, Dream Interpretation, Spirit Guides, Practical Shamanism, and Healing with Imagery. He has given monthly talks on Masonic symbolism and was a featured speaker at a special table lodge for Past Master Masons of the Area. He periodically holds evening classes in Adult literacy in Liberty Hill, for which he and his lodge were given special recognition by the Grand Masonic Lodge of Texas.*

*Jerry has held numerous community service positions, such as: Master Mason, 32 Degree Scottish Rite, York Rite Mason, Shrine, and Sigma Chi Fraternity. He and Pam are Liberty Hill Lions Club Charter Members, where both have held various offices. He is the VFW surgeon, in the Liberty Hill Chamber of Commerce and Liberty Hill P.T.A. He was President of Levis and Lace Square Dance Club for 2 years. He is a member of the American Chiropractic Association, and the Texas Chiropractic Association.*

*As a near-death experiencer, Jerry exhibited some of his poems at an IANDS convention in San Antonio.*

*A personal note: "The death experience represents the very essence, the very expression of the fabric of being. It is the ultimate of all spiritual experiences, with the only known exceptions being death itself and it's complement, birth. The numerous stories from experiencers have provided humanity with a wide variety of richness in spiritual experience. Over the ages, these tales have provided the world with the very core of spirituality, religion, and esoteric teachings. For the person who has had such an experience, it is not 'near-death.' It is a real death, both physically and psychologically. It is transformation in that it changes one's life forever. It is time to get these stories out to the public. Humanity is in need."*

*Jerry L. Casebolt, BS, DC*

Professor Charlie Young took a sip of coffee and settled back into the restaurant booth. Gary Caldwell sat across from him turning a glass of water in his hands. The turning of the glass slowed as time reversed itself. Visions of past events swiftly filtered through his mind as he gathered his thoughts.

Fort Collins, Colorado is a clean, beautiful town, snuggled in a long valley stretching from North to South. The Rocky Mountains rise abruptly and majestically just West of town. They are blue when the sun comes up. They turn shadowy dark and hide the sun before it sets. That delay produces the unparalleled beauty of Colorado sunsets and lengthy twilights. In the spring of 1948 it was an earthly paradise to the children of these mountains.

Seven-year-old Gary was not feeling well. He found it physically difficult to join the drama as the sun descended into the fiery pit in the West to be miraculously reborn the next morning in the East. Holding his stomach, he turned away and slowly went into the old farm house. His mother was preparing supper.

About half an hour later, Mr. Carl Caldwell arrived from College in the family car. He hurriedly went out to do the chores. By the time he came into the house, darkness had fallen. He was carrying an armload full of text books.

He briefly greeted his wife and four children. "Hi honey. Tests are coming up. I'm going into the bedroom to study."

"Carl, wait just a minute." She was a small, well-educated woman but highly emotional. "Gary is sick."

Carl didn't feel well himself. Suffering from pleurisy, the coughing was relentless. His tuberculosis was supposed to be in remission now but he was constantly aware of its after effects. Carl didn't have much patience these days. His stress load was more than a healthy person could tolerate. "So, what do you want me to do."

Frowning, she repeated, "Gary is sick. I would like to know what you want to do?"

Sighing with frustration and indecision, he replied, "I think he's just being a sissy. I can't even get him to go out to do the chores with me. Are you sure that he isn't just trying to get out of doing dishes, too?"

"I don't think so, Carl, his stomach is distended and it hurts him when I touch it."

Realizing that studying tonight would be difficult, he became even more perturbed. "That boy probably just needs a laxative. We haven't had our spring tonic yet this year anyway."

Now, Ada was becoming really exasperated. Her voice rose a few decibels. "Carl, you don't understand. He doesn't have any appetite."

"Ada, you worry too much. He'll be just fine." Sensing an unwanted and untimely confrontation, Carl ignored the silent frozen glare on her face. Defeated by the look, he silently turned away, and went to the bedroom to study.

By March 14, Gary was still complaining about his stomach. It was about to dawn on Mr. and Mrs. Caldwell that Gary really was sick.

Carl Caldwell was a third year student at Colorado A & M. He came home a little early that night. "Gary, get your fanny out of bed. You have come out and help me with the chores. The calf we bought together is your responsibility."

"Dad, I don't feel good. My stomach hurts."

"Come on Gary, let's get with it. Your stomach will be all right."

"I'm not fooling, Dad."

Mr. Caldwell turned and took Gary sternly by the arm. "Son, what's your problem?"

"My stomach hurts, Dad."

"It's time for some spring cleaning anyway." Mr. Caldwell was angry. "I just can't seem to teach you boys any responsibility." He released his son, turned on his heels, and headed for the barn. Throwing things around in anger, he finished the chores by himself. When he returned, he headed for the medicine cabinet. He mixed a glass of orange juice and castor oil.

"Gary, come here...Now!" commanded Mr. Caldwell in his best ex-Army voice.

"OK, OK," Gary answered, balefully.

"Oh, my goodness," thought Ada, wringing her hands in dismay. "I surely hope that man knows what he is doing. I do not have a good feeling about this at all." She knew that to express those feelings at this moment would only stir up a tired and irritated husband. She kept most of her feelings inside of herself these days.

"OK, Gary. Down the hatch," Mr. Caldwell ordered.

Gary knew better than to refuse. Down the hatch it went. Seconds later, up the hatch it came. It went everywhere.

"You did that on purpose!" reprimanded Mr. Caldwell loudly.

Gary was still choking on his vomit. "I did not, Dad."

Carl was frustrated. "Ada, come here."

Tears flowed from Ada's eyes. "What is wrong, Carl?"

Mr. Caldwell loudly replied, "I have no idea, Ada."

"Don't you think we'd better get him to the doctor tomorrow, Carl?"

"I've got to have the car tomorrow to go to school."

Ada got a wrinkled, worried face. "What if it is really something serious?"

"It isn't anything but a little colic and a bad attitude, Ada."

Ada helped Gary clean up the mess and put him to bed. Carl retired to his bedroom. Study was difficult that night, to say the least.

On the morning of March 15, Gary was too sick to get out of bed. Ada sat on the side of his bunk. "Are you all right, Gary?"

"No, Mom. I'm not."

"Maybe we can bring you a little breakfast."

"I'm not hungry, Mom. I can't eat."

"Well, you've got to eat sometime, honey."

"Not right now, Mom." Gary suddenly had a searing pain in his gut. He doubled up.

Watching, Ada's eyes brimmed with tears. Almost out loud she muttered, "What can I do?... What can I do?" Then, Ada had an inspiration. She said, "Gary, I'll be back in just a few minutes."

"Where are you going, Mom?"

"Next door to talk to Mrs. Schellenberg. She has a car and she can drive."

"Where is Dad? Why can't he take care of it?"

"He is at school taking tests, Gary. He won't be home until late tonight." Unable to hide her nervousness, Ada walked to her neighbor's house which was about a quarter of a mile East, toward town.

Meanwhile, Gary doubled over crying with pain again. He vomited up a small amount of material which smelled quite foul.

A little later, Ada came back. She seemed to be somewhat relieved. "Gary, Mrs. Schellenberg said that we may use her car and will drive you to the doctor if we have to. I called the doctor but his nurse told me that he was out of the office and will be back."

Another spasm of pain went through Gary's body. "Mom, it really hurts!"

"Can I get you some chicken noodle soup?"

"No, Mom, I told you, I'm not hungry!"

Ada noticed the stain where Gary had attempted to clean up the vomit. "What is this?" she asked.

"I don't know. It keeps coming up like this, Mom." The pain and the bloating of Gary's stomach were progressively becoming worse. Gary winced. "That's how my belly feels." Crying, he doubled up in pain again. The pain cycle lasted for about thirty minutes. For the next thirty minutes, the stomach spasms abated somewhat and he whimpered. Then, just as before, another gripping gut pain doubled him over. It repeated that cycle over and over without relief. Sleep was impossible. A kind of gray darkness enveloped him as he grew less and less aware of his surroundings. "Mom, my legs don't feel like they are there."

Ada felt of Gary's forehead. She noted the insistent rise of his temperature. Gary shivered. He became unconscious of time as the day slipped by and the intensity of pain increased.

Carl came home, did his chores and checked on Gary. Worried and sleepless, Ada checked on him several times during the night.

By the early morning of March 16, Gary welcomed the numbness. Eyes glazed over, he had gone into a kind of trance-like state sometime during the night.

"Carl, please come here. Gary's eyes don't look good."

Gary's Dad, awake from the disturbances of the night, came in the room where the boy lay doubled up in a fetal position, head extended and hands holding his lower stomach area. He saw Gary's eyes glazed over with the pain. He noted the shallow breathing. Troubled and sick himself, still unable to make a decision about it, he turned without comment and left for school.

There was much parental discussion on the night of March 16, Some of which was not very pleasant. Another sleepless, troubled night passed.

March 17 was cloudy. Ada's instincts had driven her to near frantic worry. Shortly after Carl left for school, she called the doctor's office from Mrs. Schellenberg's house. "Dr. Beebe, Gary has been sick for more than two weeks now. I don't know what to do? Will you please help me?"

"Is he holding his food down?"

"No, Sir, he vomited up some green stuff that smelled very bad."

"Does he have a fever?"

"Off and on."

"I have to make a house call right now, Mrs. Caldwell, but you need to get Gary into the office right away. My assistant will be here to help you. I will return shortly."

Mrs. Schellenberg was a stout German woman. She picked him up easily and carried him to her car. Ada was right on her heels. Gary had a puzzled look behind the pain in his face, "Where am I going, Mom?"

"To the Doctor's office. Dr. Beebe wants to take a look at you. He thinks something serious is happening." Ada wrote and handed Mrs. Schellenberg a neatly folded note. "Please give this to the doctor."

Mrs. Schellenberg put the note in her pocket, got into her car and drove away. A young doctor came out of the office. He helped Mrs. Schellenberg lift Gary out of the car and carried him into the examining room. He cried out with the pain which movement produced. They laid him on the exam table. While scrubbing down his hands, the young physician asked the woman, "Are you this boy's mother?"

"No, I'm Mrs. Schellenberg. Mrs. Caldwell is at home. I'm her neighbor. She can't leave her kids right now."

"I see. But we've got to have permission to treat him."

Mrs. Schellenberg pulled the note out of her jacket pocket and handed it over to the doctor.

He read out loud, **"Do what you can for my boy."** The note was signed and dated by Mrs. Carl Caldwell. "I think that this will do." He grinned wryly and handed the note to the nurse who promptly put it into the file.

The young doctor said, "Thanks for your trouble, Mrs. Schellenberg. You may go now, if you'd like. Tell Mrs. Caldwell we have it under control. Tell her that we will call when we know something." He turned and addressed Gary. "My name is Dr. George Bowen. We are going to do a little exam on you now." Dr. Bowen asked several pertinent questions of Gary while he checked for vital signs. He paused and made medical notations of his findings on a chart. "Now, Gary, will you show me exactly where you hurt?"

Gary pointed to his right lower stomach.

"Right about here?" Dr. Bowen asked, pressing on the indicated place.

"Yes... Yes!" Gary added the extra 'Yes' to encourage the young doctor to remove his hands a little faster.

Dr. Bowen pulled away and looked at Gary, "I'm not real sure what's going on here, Gary. Dr. Beebe will be back shortly. Maybe he can help us figure it out."

Thelma drew blood. She made a phone call. She left to take it to the hospital. Blood tests were run. Results were phoned back.

Just after lunch, Dr. Beebe came in. Thelma was with Gary cleaning up some small amounts of vomit.

"Good afternoon, Thelma. Good afternoon young man," he said looking at Gary from just outside of the exam room. "Where is Dr. Bowen?"

"He was in the other exam room just a minute ago," Thelma replied, glancing up. Seeing the younger man behind him, she offered, "I think he is right behind you, sir."

Turning around, Dr. Beebe replied, "Oh, Good afternoon, Dr. Bowen."

"Good afternoon, Sir." Dr. Bowen replied, returning the greeting to his senior.

Dr. Beebe smiled briefly at the respect shown and spoke again, "Doctor, what do you think we have here?"

"I'm not really sure sir, but I think he has appendicitis."

Dr. Bebee began his own examination. The pressure from the doctor's touch was so excruciating in the lower right abdominal area that Gary could barely stand it. Every touch brought another cry of pain.

"Ow, it really hurts." Gary managed.

"I know this hurts, son. I'll be finished in just a minute," Dr. Beebe sympathized, while probing in different parts of the intestine. In a short time, Dr. Bebee knew that it was serious.

"Gary's cry is not that of someone with appendicitis, Dr. Bowen," he said, disagreeing with the younger doctor's preliminary diagnosis. "The pain pattern is different."

Turning to Gary, he said, "I think we are going to keep you here under observation for the rest of the day, son."

At just before 8:00 p.m. on March 17, 1948, Mrs. Schellenberg received a call from Dr. Beebe. A few minutes later she walked over to her neighbor's house and knocked on the door. "Hi, Ada. I have a message from Dr. Beebe."

"Oh, my goodness," said Ada.

"It's OK. Not to worry." "See, Ada, I have it all written down on this pad." She handed Ada a pad of paper with the carefully printed message.

Ada read out loud, "MR. AND MRS. CALDWELL, WE HAVE HAD GARY UNDER OBSERVATION ALL DAY. THERE HAS BEEN NO IMPROVEMENT. WE ARE GOING TO TAKE HIM TO THE HOSPITAL FOR POSSIBLE SURGERY. PLEASE COME ON DOWN RIGHT AWAY." It was signed, "Dr. Beebe."

After necessary discussion, Mrs. Schellenberg took the three younger siblings under her wings. Mr. and Mrs. Caldwell were off to the hospital.

Meanwhile, the two doctors had simply bundled Gary up in Dr. Beebe's car who transported him.

Gary's next memory was that of lying in a hospital bed, on the second floor of Logan County Hospital in Fort Collins. There were no private rooms available. The hallways and general ward were overcrowded with patients. Gary's pajamas were traded for hospital clothes and he was placed under a single loose sheet.

Ada moved up to Gary's bed. Her eyes were wet with her constant tears. Her forehead was wrinkled with worry. Trying to be brave, she patted her son's arm and reassured him, "It is going to be all right, Gary. Everything is going to be fine." She placed her hand on his head. Ada lovingly stroked his short hair.

Carl Caldwell was silent. He was brooding and pouting. He did not seem to understand what was going on. His objections had been overruled by this emotionally distraught mother, a strange acting German neighbor woman, and an 'overreacting' physician.

Soon Dr. Beebe arrived. Another doctor tailed closely behind. Ada moved out of their way. She stationed herself next to Carl who was standing at the foot of Gary's bed. Ada took his right arm in her left. She held tightly for physical as well as psychological support.

"Good evening Mr. and Mrs. Caldwell. This is Dr. Glen Albertson who will be your surgeon." Dr. Albertson picked up the medical file and began reading the notes, ignoring the rest of the conversation.

Dr. Beebe patiently explained, "Dr. Albertson is a hospital staff surgeon, sir. Surgery is what he does. I'm a general practitioner. I will be assisting him in surgery. Be assured that Gary is in good hands, Mr. Caldwell." Dr. Bebee turned to Carl and Ada. He explained, "Our tests do not show anything unusual or abnormal, in fact they are quite inconclusive. We thought at first that it might be appendicitis, but there is too much pain for that. The white blood cells don't read right on the lab tests. They are way too low. This pattern of pain, the intermittent fever and the low white cell count suggest that he may have a severe infection. We don't know what or exactly where it is, but it looks like it is in the area of the ascending colon. You have a very sick boy here. We are recommending immediate exploratory surgery."

Dr. Albertson looked into Gary's large youthful innocent eyes. The old surgeon felt pain in his heart for the boy. He explained, "Son, we are going to go inside of you and find out what is going on."

Carl asked, "Are you going to be able to fix it, doctor?"

He turned his head. "Mr. and Mrs. Caldwell, if it is at all possible, we will get it fixed."

Like the sound of thunder in a silent tense moment, Gary softly declared, *"That means I'm going to die."*

The surgeon replied, "No, you're not, son. You're too young to die."

Gary quietly insisted, *"Yes, I am... I know I am going to die."*

Carl got a very sad look in his face. Big tears welled up in his eyes. Ada was already crying uncontrollably. Gary looked at each of them, right in their eyes, just like his Dad had taught him. He saw the doubt which they all shared. He added their reactions to the feelings deep inside of himself. That confirmed it. **Gary knew for sure that he was going to die.**

A staff nurse arrived with a hospital gurney. With pain, Gary was moved gently from the hospital bed onto it. Any remaining fear about death had completely abated. He was happy that he was about to leave this earth. The body wasn't working any more. His death was just something that he knew intuitively was coming. He did not have enough energy to argue with anyone about it. Young Gary Caldwell became silent, even thankful.

A nurse arrived, fidgeting with a syringe. "Gary, can you count to 100?"

"Yes, ma'am."

"I am going to give you this little shot," she said, holding up a needle with something in it. "I want you to count from 100 backwards."

Gary had only a little apprehension when she inserted the needle into his buttocks and pushed the plunger down, releasing the contents into his flesh. "Oooo, that burns."

"Start counting," commanded the nurse. The shot acted very quickly. It immediately put Gary into a state of euphoria. He started counting, "100, 99, 98, 97, 96, 95..." His voice trailed off to a whisper, "94, 93, 92..." Maybe his mind continued for a short time, but no more numbers left the muscles of his throat. Mind and body calmed as the shot took its effect. It was as if he could see and hear everything around him but he could not respond. His realization of impending death no longer concerned him. Pain eased as well, that is, so long as no one touched him or caused any part of his body to wiggle.

A male nurse roughly moved the gurney into the hallway. The movement brought a cry of pain from the nearly unconscious child. It was from this abrupt movement that Gary suddenly realized that he was *no longer in his body*. A part of him was now hovering in the air, watching his own body. His gurney was in the hall, now the first in a lineup of three gurneys awaiting surgery. From his advantage of height, he observed his Mom and Dad sitting on a hard bench on the other side of the hospital corridor. Sorrowfully, Carl sat leaning forward with his hat in his hands between his knees. Staring into space, he waved it up and down by the brim in short, nervous strokes. Ada sat beside him, clinging to his right arm, crying and worrying. They talked little to each other.

A nurse pushed open the double doors. Everyone watched as she pulled the gurney into the operating room. Gary saw the movement and followed in his spirit body. Skillful hands transferred his physical body to the operating table. Someone pushed the gurney toward the double doors. Gary's attention followed the movement from a position near the ceiling. It hit the doors, bounced loudly against them, then rolled backwards. Working in silence, a wise old nurse scrubbed and applied iodine to the body's stomach. Gary observed two large surgical reflector lights shining down on the operating area. There were tubes and wires hooked up to his body. He observed the trays of surgical instruments. There were two doctors and two nurses working. Another person looked after the ether. Maybe he was a doctor too.

A mask with a hose on it was applied to the face. Valves were turned on. Ether came through the mask. The face winced from the smell. A strange humming began. The walls had a green cast. Everything shimmered with it's own energy. *"I haven't really died,"* Gary thought. *"If death is this simple, it's really no big deal."*

Moving around in the room, he tried to turn some of the knobs on the instruments in the operating area. Try as he might, he could not manipulate the knobs, valves or buttons. "It is a good thing too," it occurred to him, "I might accidentally kill myself." He chuckled at himself.

Skillfully one doctor made the incision. Blood oozing, Gary decided that it was much more fun seeing through the walls, moving about through halls, watching patients, and doing just about anything you can imagine. Freedom was really great fun! He simply could not get over the idea that *there was no more pain.*

Suddenly, Gary sensed an emergency. He swiftly returned to the operating room. At first, he had difficulty figuring out what was happening then he perceived that it had something to do with his breathing.

Alarm and agitation replaced euphoria. The anesthesiologist wasn't paying attention to what he was doing. He was watching the surgeons rather than minding his own business. Too much ether was being released. The body was in deep trouble.

"Stop! Turn it off," Gary yelled. He paused, thought for a moment and changed his mind. "Leave it alone. Let it die. It isn't any good anymore. Let it go!" No one responded. They didn't seem to hear a word he was saying.

Gary thought, "This is stupid. It is next too impossible to talk to someone who is dead. No, it is next to impossible to talk to someone who is alive!" Not only did that realization frustrate him, but it also fascinated him. Then he lost interest in the crisis. "Oh, well, let them work," he thought, "even if it is a waste of time."

Something else was going wrong. The energy in his physical body was beginning to decrease. The colors in the room began to dim. Apprehension enveloped him. He lost his sense of time and movement. The past and future began to fuse right in front him.

Gary distinctly remembered saying, earlier in the day, *"I'm going to die."* Gary knew that his Dad was going to have to sell a cow in order to pay for this operation. He remembered watching those thoughts pass through his Dad's mind. It was as if he could still see the image of those thoughts. "If I die, Dad won't have to sell that cow because there won't have to be an operation. But, now there's going to be an operation and I'm going to die anyway."

Alarmed, one of the doctors muttered to the others, *"Something is wrong."*

The intensity of the humming sound increased in Gary's ears.

There was an immediate flurry of activity in the operating room. Dr. Albertson said, *"I think we are losing him.* What's his blood pressure?"

"I can't get it," replied one of the nurses.

Gary thought, "That's a stupid thing to say. *I'm not lost,* I'm right up here."

Dr. Beebe took over the blood pressure duties from the nurse. He felt for the return of a pulse. "It's weak but it's back." With more urgency, the operating crew continued with their medical tasks.

Gary realized that he really had a great desire to stay in this present spirit state. It was just like dreams, except it was real. He could see himself as energy and light. *"I'm free,"* he thought.

Once again Gary focused attention on the body. He could see inside the cut which extended from the navel to the pubic bone. As the doctors began to uncover the different parts, they saw simultaneously what Gary saw. The gut was stuck inside of itself.

Dr. Albertson murmured, "shit, gangrene. This kid is in deep trouble. This is a telescoped bowel."

Gary didn't know what that word, 'telescoped bowel' meant, but he understood what the word 'shit' meant. There was another flurry of activity in the operating room.

Dr. Albertson commented, "I've only seen this one other time in all the years that I've been doing surgery."

They continued working on the gut, carefully pulling it apart. The gangrenous part was cut out. The remaining parts of the gut were sewn back together.

Another shift in the energy dimmed the room. A voice announced, "There goes his blood pressure again!" With finality, another voice said, *"**He's gone! Move it.**"*

Gary lost track of the frantic activity as transparent electric tension filled the operating room. The colors in the room faded to a dull gray-black. Swirling energy patterns drew Gary's attention to the North West area of the operating room. It roared as it formed a tunnel, pulling him toward its center. The sound resembled that of a jet engine when you stand next to it. Gary felt great fear, maybe terror.

The initial terrifying sound and Gary's fear abated. He became aware of a Being of Light with him in the tunnel. He had been aware of the presence of this Being earlier but didn't make much of it. Now the situation was different. The Light Being had great dark eyes. It appeared as if there was an outline of a shadowy body within the Light body. He felt the depth of the love the Light Being had for him.

The tunnel in which the travelers moved could change its size or Gary could change his size. Learning came rapidly. The inside surface revolved clockwise, swirling in waves of alternating gray-black to gray-white colors. *Extraordinary events had become ordinary.*

Moving further inward, Gary thought, "I know you." The Light Being acknowledged Gary's recognition instantly. Gary thought, "Maybe I've seen you in my dreams." The energy of the Light Being beamed with a smile-like radiance. Thought communication with the Being was accomplished in a marvelous and most mysterious way. In this reality, words are apparently transmitted by some form of intent.

A miniature thought-picture assembled itself in the upper area of the Light Being. As the picture intensified, a kind of humming sound started in Gary's head. The humming sound began to increase as the intensity and detail of the thought-picture in the Light Being increased. Just a few milliseconds later the thought-picture suddenly transmitted from the Light Being into Gary's head. The humming then ceased.

When Gary gave an answer, his thought-answer began with a similar humming sound in his head as his own miniature thought-picture formed. In an instant that thought-picture transferred into the head of the Light Being.

"Is it an angel? If it is, it doesn't have any wings. It doesn't need any." The Light Being patiently gave Gary instant thought-answers to each of his questions.

Gary thought, "I don't have any wings either. I'm made out of light, just like the other Being. Look how easy it is to move now. I'm flying. Boy, this isn't like anything I learned about in Church. Someone must have made a lot of that stuff up."

The movement through the tunnel accelerated. They continuously read and answered each other's thoughts. Gary could feel the gentle and understanding humor as he worked out the perceptions in this world.

Gary instinctively knew that he had come to this earth through this same tunnel. *He had been here before.* He thought, "Maybe this is the way all beings pass between the worlds."

The end of the tunnel was not visible because it appeared to have a bend in it. As the two travelers turned slightly to the right at the bend, *Gary saw a small Light at the end of the tunnel,* which seemed to grow larger as they approached.

With a sense of anticipation and urgency, the two companions arrived at the end of the tunnel in *no time* at all. It became amazingly apparent that the only requirement for anything, including movement, was simple intent.

When they arrived at the end of the tunnel, a Light Being of even greater brilliance met Gary. This Light Being was situated just to the left of the tunnel. The first Being mysteriously disappeared.

Totally enraptured, Gary thought, "It doesn't have a body. It is just Light." The Light from this Being was more powerful than the sun, but Gary's eyes were able to look directly at it. He became very still and watched this Great Light Being in silent awe. It had the most unforgettable eyes that one could imagine. They were like deep black coals of piercing fire. If this Being had a name, Gary failed to think about asking what it was.

This Great Light Being greeted Gary like a long lost friend. He felt complete confidence in the Light Being. *Gary felt the embrace of incredible love, peace, and ecstatic bliss.* His own Light Body tingled all over like a sparkle wand. The ecstatic feeling permeated the very core of his Being. He felt like he had been given the gift of seeing the very center of the great mystery, the indefinable, the infinite. There was the feeling of knowing something undeniably and eternally truthful. Yet, there was the feeling that there was much to see and learn.

The Great Light Being wanted Gary to communicate from his heart. All of the past, present and future fused into one single moment of existence as Gary responded with thought-pictures. It did not seem to care about any religion or doctrine. There was no vengeful god waiting and it did not want anything from Gary. There was no King-of-the Dead sitting on any throne, and there was no vengeful judgment.

This was a place of most incredible beauty, the epitome of everything imaginable.

The Great Light Being transmitted thought-pictures and instructions. They were going on a *grand tour.* The two Lights moved into another world. On the left Gary noticed what seemed to be a swampy, hazy area. It was a pleasant place. There was a watery substance in front of them. It was still, reflective, murky, and primordial.

The Great Light Being was suddenly on the other side of the watery substance. Experiencing apprehension, Gary hesitated. As he relaxed, stepping stones magically rose out of the water. The Great Light Being warned him to be careful and not to step off the stones and into the water.

Gary thought, "There might be great danger if I step into that water." On the other hand, he knew instinctively that he should continue his journey.

The Light Being watched patiently as Gary worked out the details. He first thought, "Stepping on the stones without slipping off is going to be difficult."

Stepping tentatively, Gary discovered that it wasn't difficult at all. With each step, his confidence returned. Any residual fear was totally gone by the time he reached the other side.

Gary's attention was drawn to his left. There amongst the shadows of the trees and the haze, were those entities that may be referred to as *"the dead."* They appeared as light forms standing in small groups under majestic trees growing upon an island.

Gary recognized them as friends and relatives who had already passed this way. He especially recognized his Grandmother, who had passed to this side of the veil-of-memory in the same year that he was born. Ada had shown him a number of pictures of her mother and her funeral. He recognized many other shadowy Entities as his friends from the dream world.

They appeared to be engrossed in deep but animated conversation. When they saw Gary, they became excited. They waved and smiled with recognition. Gary grinned with understanding and excitement, but passed on.

The adventure then led him into the very depths of the inner worlds. He was able to experience all the possibilities which intent allowed. The scenes and the Beings in this place were simply indescribable in words that are found in our Earthly language.

Gary experienced feelings of joy, awe, confidence, and incredible beauty. The surreal colors shifted endlessly. He explored endless worlds of indescribable beauty. He transmitted messages to other Beings. They transmitted messages to him. He watched reality change instantaneously before his senses. Sounds of music pervaded this paradisiacal place. Gary listened and learned. He gained a sense of an eternal connection which was never to leave his waking consciousness.

Gary received no messages or prophecies to bring back except the story itself. But, he was permanently instilled with a different perception of what life really is.

Unexpectedly, there was a roaring sound. Just as if the two travelers had not really traveled anywhere, the tunnel simply and incomprehensibly reformed. Dazed, Gary sent the thought-question, "What is the tunnel doing here?"

The voice of the Great Light Being transmitted, "**YOU HAVE TO GO BACK NOW.**"

"NO... NO," Gary argued, "That is an old dead body down there. I'm not going back."

"**YOU HAVE TO GO BACK,**" repeated the Great Light Being.

"Why do I have to go back?"

"**BECAUSE YOU HAVE WORK TO DO!**" the sound picture boomed.

That phrase "**BECAUSE YOU HAVE WORK TO DO,**" reverberated painfully in his light body.

"I'm not going back there," he argued.

"**You have to go back.**"

"No... no."

Further argument was not forthcoming from the Light Being. With almost a wistful kindness, it simply but powerfully booted Gary down the tunnel. Down and down he went. "Aaaa..." His insides were screaming. He thought, "No, No, No... this can't be!" "Why can't I stay here?" It felt like spiraling down an old fashioned fire escape tunnel like they used to have at schools just after World War II.

Disoriented, Gary landed in the open sky somewhere above Fort Collins, Colorado. It was sunny, about the middle of the morning. He spotted the original Light Being who had escorted him through the tunnel. With a little help, Gary spotted the hospital. They flew there together. Hovering, he noticed that the roof was flat with short walls on the sides. There were noisy machines on the roof. Maybe they were air handling equipment. Gary could see through the hospital roof, but, at the same time, it felt solid enough for support.

He spotted the body on the second floor of the hospital. It was on the East side near the center of the ward. Gary was a little surprised that the body was even on the ward. He had left it in the operating room. He felt as if he had been gone for three or four days, evidently because of the amount of perceptions which had occurred in the other worlds. On the other hand, it may have been much less time, maybe even for just a few minutes. It was a mystery. "How could it be morning? It was at night, dark, when I left here," he thought. Gary noticed that Dr. Beebe and his Dad were standing near the body but he wasn't particularly interested in what was transpiring.

Floating just above the roof, he moved to the North end of the building. There was a school just North of the Hospital. Between the buildings, there was a playground filled with sand and lots of children. It had teeter-totters, slides, and ropes mounted on bars from which to swing.

A German Shepard dog was playing with the children. Gary floated down to investigate. The dog sensed his presence and playfully barked at him. At first the children didn't take notice because they were absorbed in their own play.

Gary floated down and positioned himself just a few inches above where the dog could jump. He teased the animal by staying just out of reach. The dog barked and jumped up at Gary. As the dog became more excited, the children took notice. One small girl began to cry. Others looked around for the cause of the disturbance. The dog continued to wag his tail excitedly, barking and jumping crazily up at Gary. Gary laughed. He was having a good time like any seven-year-old kid should.

The Light Being did not share in the humor of the moment. It stopped this 'childish' diversion and hauled Gary back to the top of the hospital roof as it transmitted, "You are causing the other children to be frightened."

"They don't even know that I'm here."

"You have to go back into your body now."

"But," he argued, "It is a dead body. I'm not interested in it. I want to spend the rest of my *'life'* the way I am right now."

The Light Being simply watched while Gary argued.

Dr. Beebe was now standing on the right side of the body. His father was standing directly behind the doctor.

Pointing to his body, Gary said to the Light Being, "Look, Dr. Beebe is raising my eyelids. He thinks I'm dead, too." The Light Being smiled patiently.

With a penlight, Dr. Beebe periodically looked into the eyes each time he opened an eyelid. Gary sensed the physician's displeasure. The doctor muttered discouraging words to Carl who sorrowfully shook his head. Exhausted, Ada was standing at the foot of the bed.

Gary said to the Light Being, "I could tell the doctor that I'm not in there." The Light Being gestured in such a way as to encourage Gary to be patient and watch for a minute.

Carl's mind was whirling, "God, I'm afraid. If there is a funeral, how am I going to pay for it. How am I ever going to finish school?"

Emotions swirled in and around both his Dad and Mom while Dr. Beebe voiced his foreboding in the prescribed medical manner.

"How am I going to live with Ada if Gary doesn't make it?" thought Carl. His hands were shaking. His heart was beating fast. He kept pulling out a handkerchief and spitting foul stuff into it then folding it over and replacing it into his back pocket.

But another drama drew Gary's attention to the North end of the ward. The nurse's station was situated here. The door to the station was in the Northeast corner of the upper level.

Just to the left of the door to the nurse's station was a bed with an old lady in it. Two, maybe three, overstuffed pillows supported her frail skinny body. She had long, white, stringy hair. The ends stood up as if she had been shocked by an electric cattle prod. She yelled, "I hurt... I hurt. I'm too hot!"

Used to the disturbance, the nurses ignored her.

A moment later she yelled again, "I'm too cold! I'm hungry! I hurt!"

Curiously observing, Gary moved toward her body, "She isn't even in there. She must have been gone for a long time." He felt concern for the discomfort which her behavior was continually causing the other patients. "Old lady, you're a phony. You are yelling but you can't feel pain." Her body was made noises but her mind wasn't there.

A blood pressure cuff was permanently installed upon her left arm. To her left and above her head, the mercury bulb was securely hung on the wall. Just in front of that was a rolling medical stand. Intravenous tubes connected the old woman to her bottled life support. Some were hooked up to her left arm, some to her right. An oxygen mask hung loosely over her face, barely muffling her loud complaints.

Gary sensed an urgent need to help out the agitated patients. Some were startled when she yelled out unexpectedly. She waked some of them up from fitful sleep. They mumbled to the nurse or each other about not being able to get any rest.

That did it. Gary felt obligated to "fix the problem." He floated over to her bed. He tried tickling her nose with his finger. Surprisingly, after a few attempts, Gary appeared to be successful. To her, it may have felt like a feather or a chilly breeze, but to Gary it was a finger. Reflexively, it made her sneeze. As long as she was sneezing, she wasn't hollering. Gary was amused with himself and the patients welcomed the change, at least at some level. Several of them sighed with temporary relief from the noise.

A dark haired young man, a veteran of World War One, was sitting beside his bed in a chair. The name, 'Billy Chadwick' was on his chart. He was unsuccessfully trying to read a book. Watching and noting the change at the end of the ward, he thought he sensed something unusual in the atmosphere. Shaking his head back and forth, he chuckled.

The Light Being did not approve of Gary's 'childish' antics any more than the incident with the dog. It turned Gary away from the old lady and sternly transmitted "That is enough."

Feeling the irritation emanating from the Light Being, Gary failed to understand why. He moved toward his body in the bed but hesitated. Something strange began to happen. An unusual energy brightened the atoms and molecules of his flesh. Apparently something or someone was healing the body. Gary couldn't figure out what the source was.

Seconds after that happened, his companion, the Light Being, simply took Gary by the spiritual scruff of his neck and pushed him down the center aisle and put him back into his body.

In the same instant, Dr. Beebe pulled up the right eyelid to see if Gary was in there. He recognized the change of life-signs in the eyes and nodded his head up and down as if he knew exactly what was happening. Gary's eyes came open and looked up at Dr. Beebe. The Doctor exclaimed, looking at Gary, *"Boy, I am sure glad you're back. We thought we had lost you."*

*"Would you like to know where I've been?"* Gary asked, tentatively.

Embarrassed by the boy's reply, the physician replied, *"No, not really."*

Gary ignored the negative tone and began to talk anyway. **"I've been to heaven... I got to see the face of God..."** Gary glanced at the blank, unbelieving faces around him. It was as if he could read their minds. He realized, "They are not listening. They are afraid!"

The doctor turned and spoke to Mr. Caldwell. "He is just hallucinating. You can easily see that, can't you?" He explained.

Mr. Caldwell nodded his head halfway in agreement, "I really don't know what to think."

Gary insisted, "I am not hallucinating!"

"Please, settle down, son. You are still seriously ill."

"I feel fine," Gary argued, defensively.

Dr. Beebe and Mr. Caldwell both nervously backed away into the center aisle. Their eyes were shifting back and forth. They would not look at Gary or at each other. He read their thoughts, "He may not be in his right mind."

Gary's Mom was crying again but for happy reasons now. She didn't care about anything else. His Dad moved back to hold her by the shoulders. Mr. Caldwell whispered, "Why are you crying? He's going to be all right."

"I know," was all she was able to verbalize.

Now Gary was crying, but it wasn't evident. Gary's cry was one of silent disappointment in the humans around him. He felt desperate, "I want to tell them where I have been. I can't understand why they don't want to hear about it. Everyone should be happy to know about my adventure with the Light Beings." At his deepest core, like a compulsion, Gary knew that the story had to be told. But, the more he insisted on talking about it, the more upset everyone became. Gary perceived that they were actually afraid of stories from Paradise. "Why?" he asked himself. Frustrated with the frailty of his parent's beliefs, he wisely decided to hold the experience silently in his heart.

Attempting to reassure everyone, Dr. Beebe said, "He'll be all right. We'll get something to calm him down."

Gary's silence had a calming effect. Still nervous, he silently observed these intelligent human adults in the throes of their own internal struggles which they projected into their perceptions.

He perceived Dr. Beebe's thoughts. "I wonder if this kid has some brain damage. He doesn't have any other symptoms of it though. Maybe we'll test him later on."

Gary thought, "You shouldn't think things like 'brain damage' around a kid like me." He let the doctor's thoughts pass.

Carl shook his head back and forth. He thought, "I'm sick. I don't know what is going on. I really don't know what to think."

Ada was happy. She was relieved. She thought, "I don't know what the fuss is all about, I'm just happy that Gary is alive."

Making a decision, Dr. Beebe called out, "Nurse!"

A nurse near the North end of the ward answered, "Yes, Sir?"

"Let's give Gary an injection of Morphine to calm him down. We need to sedate him. He is *hallucinating*."

Gary thought but dared not voice aloud, "*I am not hallucinating! You are the one that is hallucinating!*"

Addressing the doctor, the nurse said, "Yes, Sir," and hurried back to the station. She returned and gave Gary the injection. The liquid stung when it entered his buttocks. Losing consciousness, Gary happily drifted out of his body. "Now I can go back to the other side," he dreamed.

It was not to be. The Light Being became visible once more. Gary was able to briefly communicate with it but he was unable to get back into the tunnel. He drifted in and out of his body. The Light Being disappeared into the darkness of the drug-induced semi-unconsciousness. Gary sank into the miserable realization that he was back in earth's bonds to stay for a while. The memory of the booming voice echoed from the other side, "***YOU HAVE WORK TO DO.***"

"How could that make any sense to a seven-year-old kid?" Gary thought. Deep sadness and anger overwhelmed him. "How can I know what this **'WORK'** is. The stupid way everyone is reacting, I don't even really care about being here."

Now the experience was etched permanently in Gary's mind, but time would eventually change his perception about it.

Thought pictures continually floated in and out of both his waking and sleeping dreams. He remembered how incredible and unbelievably beautiful it was in the other worlds... and, at the same time, the veil-of-memory slowly but only partially slipped over his mind.

Gary woke up in the night. He saw no familiar faces. There were, of course, the other patients on the ward and the nurse. She was a different person than the one who had been there earlier. She busied herself making up beds and performing the many hospital chores. When she came by Gary's bed, he volunteered, "Would you like to hear about my trip to heaven?"

In a deep feminine voice, she replied, "Sure, honey." She was hurrying to get her work done, but Gary didn't pay any attention to her mild agitation.

"Please listen, I've got to tell someone," Gary told her. Without waiting for permission, he commenced telling her the story. The nurse continually repeated, "It'll be OK honey." At one point, she interjected, "Would you like another pain shot?"

Indignantly, Gary replied, "No... I don't hurt! I just want to talk." She listened for a little while longer then interrupted, "Come on honey, let's get quiet now. You need to sleep. You're gonna need your strength." The nurse kept patting his head.

Defeated, Gary asked her, "When can I leave and go home?" She glanced at his medical chart. She smiled warmly, "I shouldn't tell you this but when you've had a good bowel movement, you will probably get to leave." Her warm hand felt good to Gary's forehead. He thought, "I wish that she would leave her hand right there and listen to my story."

Gary drifted back into a fitful sleep, thinking about her warm touch, bowel movements, the tunnel and the Great Light Being. The memories gave him a warm feeling. Dreaming was the best he could do for now.

A few days later, Gary reported to Dr. Beebe's office. Thelma removed the stitches. She kissed him on the forehead. "I'm happy that you decided to stay with us."

Gary blushed, smiled a toothy smile, and refrained from answering.

The doctors and the Light Beings had done a good job. Gary's body was young and resilient. He quickly healed and his strength rebounded.

The 'Lights' faded in Colorado. Gary was mentally back in the booth in the restaurant, slowly turning his glass of water, bringing time back to the present. Tears in his eyes, Charlie sat looking at Gary in silence. Gary softly said, "and that is the story of how a young boy was *refused at Heaven's Gate.*"

In the years that followed, Gary had many spiritual and physical experiences just like every other soul on this Earth. Some were negative and some positive. For every experience, there is a good story. In old age when the truth of life is in question, the only thing left is the STORY. The more stories that can be told, the more likely one might have some inkling of the truth.

That experience in 1948 influenced Gary's life but influenced it in many wonderful ways. Learning from the school of hard knocks, he eventually discovered that his "WORK" was in helping other people. His service is given with love and humor. And that is the way it is today.

*Jerry Casebolt*

# A Single Tear

*Donna DeSoto experienced near-death. This story explains how it changed her life. She now runs Sav-Baby, a nonprofit organization to prevent abandonment of newborn babies and young children.*

In 1983, during a near-death episode, I promised to "do something" for children in exchange for my life.

My husband and I thus foster-adopted Ben, only hours old when he was abandoned by his birth mother. At first, I felt hostile towards a woman who would abandon such a beautiful child. I felt that she must have been a horrible person. In time, however, my feelings softened. I think she cared. She had a note pinned on him that said, "Please take care of him. He needs you. I need you."

Adopting Ben turned my thoughts to fulfilling that earlier promise, toward helping abandoned babies. Another San Antonio family had adopted an abandoned baby girl.

I was to meet soon with the adoptive family to discuss a germ of an idea to help throwaway infants.

Another newborn baby girl had been found stuffed into a plastic bag and thrown into someone's front yard like a piece of trash. The child died.

Without an adoption, dead abandoned babies are destined for paupers' graves. The adoptive family was moved to adopt this child, too, in order to give her the only thing left to offer—a "proper" burial with a "real" name. So, although the adoptive family's new baby had been with them just a few weeks, they adopted this other baby. So, though we had a planned meeting already, the funeral would intervene.

Because I could not find a baby-sitter for my two sons, there I was with Ben in my arms and my four year old—Robert—standing at the graveside of this abandoned baby, this baby not as fortunate as Ben. Robert stood at the edge of the dead baby's grave.

I glanced at Robert only to witness a tear fall from his face. I saw that tear drop right into the grave. For weeks after that, I'd wake up in a cold sweat, shaking. I could not get that image out of my mind.

Seeing Robert's tear fall into that dead baby's grave pushed me closer still to the mission I had promised. I was just an everyday homemaker and housewife until then. I knew something had to be done but wasn't quite sure how to do anything. The funeral of this little girl is why Sav-Baby was founded, a non-profit agency launched with a candlelight service in 1991.

I held a press conference in my front yard to announce the start of the first organization in the country to prevent the abandonment of newborn babies and to protect their legal rights. I founded SAV-BABY October 22, 1991 and incorporated July 22nd, 1992. I installed a 1-800 toll-free hotline out of my own money hoping to reach girls before they got desperate enough to abandon their babies.

This organization has grown wildly. In one year, SAV-BABY has been on five national talk shows, on local and national news. A Hollywood producer and his crew from the Home Show came to San Antonio for three days to film a show about SAV-BABY.

The ensuing years have given me more compassion for mothers who abandon their babies. I don't totally understand what leads them to do it. Most are normal people but they crack. There was a case of a 47-year-old who denied her pregnancy even after delivery and tying the umbilical cord. She abandoned the baby, went to a store to buy cat food and went home to fix dinner.

Some mothers think they are leaving their infants in good locations, but there is no safe place to abandon a baby. Although I think that Ben's birth mother meant well, the child had been bleeding for hours where his umbilical cord had been ripped away.

The organization is set up to refer and intervene where appropriate. Hotline volunteers can aid clients directly or seek resources that can help. Sometimes I have brought girls into my own home.

Cases that come my way run the gamut from mild to extreme. One woman who had required months of assistance saw me on a talk show and called SAV-BABY. She had two small children in diapers, a newborn on a heart monitor and pregnant with a fourth child. The home was so filthy that it took volunteers four days to clean it. The children had been in the same diapers for days and the family's clothes were so dirty and moldy that they had to be thrown out. Cockroaches were everywhere.

SAV-BABY coordinated several volunteer agencies to help the woman get her life in order. I have no idea how many people have been helped by the organization. But it has worked on at least thirty serious cases this past year. I am passionate about my work to prevent infant abandonment. God drove me to do this. I made a promise and He's helped me keep it.

*Donna DeSoto*

# n Tears

*Born in Houston, September 17th, 1965, Gabriel Santiago attended private Catholic schools throughout his academic career. Gabriel is a published poet and currently working on his own collection of poems. Presently an assistant manager at the Antique Center of Texas in Houston, he also enjoys restoring antiques. His greatest treasure, though, is his intimate relationship with Jesus and God the Father. He cherishes his family and Cadi—his wife to be—as they make the rest of their stay here in this world a joyous one.*

> *"One day as he was praying in solitude, Jesus Christ appeared to him, hanging on the cross. He made Francis realize so vividly the force of his Gospel words, 'If any man has a mind to come my way, let him renounce self, and take up his cross, and follow me' (Mt 16, 24) that his heart was filled with compassion and burned within him with the fire of love. His soul melted at the sight of the vision, and the memory of Christ's passion was impressed so intimately on the depths of his heart that the wounds of his crucified Lord seemed to be always before his mind's eye, and he could scarcely restrain his sighs and tears. Now that he no longer had any regard for all that he owned in the world, and thought nothing of it for love of Jesus Christ, Francis felt that he had found the hidden treasure, the brilliant pearl of great price, mentioned in the Gospel."[1]*

On January 2, 1990, I went into the hospital for back surgery. The night before I was lying in bed listening to the fireworks outside my window. I remember thinking "What a way to start the New Year." I sure hoped the rest of the decade went a lot better. After six months of severe pain, I really didn't have any options.

---

1 St. *Francis of Assisi Writings and Early Biographies—English Omnibus of the Sources for the Life of St. Francis* (Quincy, Illinois, 1991), p. 795.

My only choice was surgery or I would live with this debilitating pain for the rest of my life. Needless to say I was very afraid.

There were so many unanswered questions. Would everything be all right? What about my Mother and Father? What about my brother Abel? What about the business I was about to start? You see, my mother and father weren't getting any younger, and my brother Abel is retarded and ill. At that time I was doing a lot of the care-giving for them. The business I was eager to start was now going to be put on hold for at least a year. Even after a year's time there was no guarantee that I could physically do the job. If I couldn't do it physically, then what was I to do? These questions and fears were only the tip of the iceberg, there were so many more. It all weighed very heavily on me.

I spent the days prior to surgery in a great deal of anxiety. When I wasn't praying I was crying; and when I wasn't crying I was praying. Everything during this time in my life was very full of fear and very hard to accept.

I went into surgery that morning, and by the grace of God, everything went well. The love and support of my family made my hospital stay much easier to cope with. Four days later I was allowed to come home. I remember thinking about the full year of recovery to come. What a waste of valuable time, I thought. I just couldn't understand why God would allow this in my life, it wasn't as if I didn't have enough crosses to carry. Thinking of this left me very dumbfounded. I tried my best not to be angry with God. I knew this was not a punishment, but it sure was hard to see it as a blessing. In my resentment to God I prayed less and cried more. Coming home was hard, because it marked the start of the long recovery that I wasn't looking forward to.

It was now three weeks after my back surgery. I was getting ready for bed that night and an end to my recovery seemed an eternity away. I went to sleep tired of everything, tired of praying, tired of crying, and tired of waiting. From what seemed like my normal unconscious state of sleep, I slowly gained consciousness. It was as if I were wide awake, and for all practical purposes I thought I was. "Where am I?" I thought. I found myself standing in clouds. They swirled all around me in large circles. I didn't know how I got there and I thought that odd. I looked out into the distance in front of me and could see a figure of a man walking towards me. All I could tell from that distance is that He was wearing a long white robe. Suddenly, like a ton of bricks hitting me, I was very surprised to see that it was Jesus. "Jesus! What's Jesus doing here?" I thought. Very lightly I started to feel emotional pain, but I didn't know or understand why. Jesus continued to walk towards me, getting closer with each step. Closer now, I could see His face clearer, and to my great disbelief, He was crying. In an instant, that little pain I was feeling earlier, exploded into a tremendous emotional hurt. Clearer still, I could see His face. It had the appearance of white stone. Despite its rock appearance, His face moved. His expressions were made with more intensity than you or I could ever show. He cried bitterly, all the tears I shed prior to this night were nothing compared to the loving crushing state He was in. Tears rolled down His face endlessly, His sobbing shook His entire body as He slowly raised His hands to cover His face in pain. All about His presence He was lit brightly, it seemed as if sparks of light showered out before Him. Waves of tremendous compassion passed through me in incredible proportions. My heart melted. I cried beyond all my control. I couldn't even maintain myself to stay standing. I fell to whatever ground there was. The feelings of His compassion and love were crushing me to a state far beyond comprehension. Unable to lift my head, I slowly raised my eyes to see Him standing in front of me. I didn't think it possible to feel any more love, compassion, and sorrow, but as I looked into His eyes I dropped into another and much deeper well of excruciating love. As He cried in this love and sorrow, it tore my heart in two. "What is Jesus doing crying?" I thought. "What is the King of The Universe doing crying?" I was lost in my bewilderment. Amidst all our tears, He looked into my eyes, and as if through telepathy He said,

*"MY CHILDREN, THEIR ACTIONS AND CHOICES ARE LEAVING THEM NO HEAVEN TO GAIN."*

The very next thing I remember I was opening my eyes. I found myself lying in bed. The sun was shining gloriously through the windows of my room. I was in the sweetest peace I've ever known. My body felt wonderfully pain free and rested. I lay there quiet, breathing in the sweet morning. From out of this glorious peace, I began to think, something very incredible had just happened. I thought that if this were a dream it was the most realistic and intense dream I had ever had. I knew then and there, I would never be the same, my life would forever be altered.

For the following three weeks, I experienced the greatest peace I've ever known. I found being outdoors to be overwhelmingly beautiful. The grand blue sky was magnificent to behold. It seemed that the sun bathed my face warm and lovingly. The wind so fresh and cool, would fill my lungs with life. My nights were spent in heavenly sleep. Prior to that experience, my life was in the worst state it had ever been in, and now, literally overnight, peace and joy encompassed me. A peace so strong I thought that nothing could ever disturb it.

Unfortunately, my return to the world would eventually happen, and gradually the bliss and peace faded. I went through an unbearable longing for heaven. Many a night I lay in bed with a longing for God that was very strong. It was so strong that I often thought there might be something wrong with me. In my ignorance I was unable to find the words to tell anyone what I was feeling, for I wasn't sure myself. Time and time again I would remember that night, going back to it so desperately, longing to return. What happened to me? What is this? Why have I changed?

I began to search for answers. I was led sometimes gently and sometimes through experiences of synchronicity that were so incredible that even my family who witnessed them, found it astonishing. Many times in these instances all I could do was cry in wonderment, for I could see a Divine Providence at work in my life. That one year recovery time went by very fast as my everyday life was now filled with God.

Five years later, it's been a wonderful passage of time. I'm constantly learning, constantly growing, and constantly my true self is being revealed. By the grace of God life goes on. In both good times and bad, those words told to me echo in the depths of my heart. Always they bring to me a certain knowledge of God's love for us, and aid me in my choices. For our God, in His infinite wisdom and love, does not force Himself upon us. In His immense love, He gives us free will. The choices, good or bad, are ours to make.

In putting my story to paper, I found that to draw any conclusions in the middle of retelling it, would disturb the story itself. The truth and the love of God allow me to make a statement concerning the one thing that Jesus revealed to me as He spoke those words. I do not wish to sound as if I am preaching, it is my farthest intention to do that. I ask for your forgiveness if it sounds that way. I merely wish to state a fact that I have come to understand. "My children, their actions and choices are leaving them no heaven to gain..." These words he spoke were born of infinite compassion. That tremendous pain was born out of an infinite amount of love, because it hurt Him so much that we were only hurting ourselves. By our own free will we choose in all circumstances. Many choices are made out of fear, many out of ease, most out of selfishness. I myself am striving for choices made out of a healthier balance of grace, love and logic. For ever since that night five years ago, my heart has been changed. Compassion has done wonders for the cold spots that used to dwell there. These are some of the results of seeing Jesus crying. If you saw Him begging, pleading and crying in that total loving compassion, you couldn't help pursue a life of a more perfect love. There was no trace of a God condemning anyone, only a God of love, pleading—in tears.

*Gabriel B. Santiago*

# Emerging

*Richard Trask is a general contractor.*

In the nearly 29 years since my transforming (near-death) event, I have come to believe that we are truly spiritual beings who have chosen to participate in the life experience on earth. The intent of the experience, as near as I can tell, is to have fun while learning through embracing the evolutionary dance of duality in the physical universe.

We are given egos for protection and survival while we are in the physical realm. The purpose of ego, then, is only for living. I believe our spirit sheds the ego when it departs the physical universe.

But ego also blocks our channels to spiritual knowing and Creation. This is why a moment in the flesh without an ego can be such an epiphany. With ego death, the channels to our Creator are opened and we are swept away for an instant by that presence, a presence where all-knowing dwells. It is an experience that is as unique to each of us as the uniqueness of a snowflake, and it melts just as quickly (but it leaves its own indelible print on our individual psyche). If there is a common thread that binds all these individual epiphanies together, I believe it is the overwhelming experience of unconditional love. Love is the manifestation of our Creator through our spiritual being. George Lucas calls it "The Force." If it is not the only true force in or out of existence, then it is undeniably, the driving and, by far, the most powerful force in the universe.

I was having a great time until I suddenly realized I was going to drown.

Until that moment, I had thought we were about to have a picnic at the "other place." The "other place" was across the

Arkansas River, but still a part of my paternal grandparents' farm, just east of Pueblo, Colorado. Pop (my grandfather) had hitched the team to the hay wagon, loaded up the family and headed for the river.

Pop was a true master horseman. In his younger days he had made a good part of his cash income by "breaking" plow teams. My father often said that Pop did most of the plowing on the farm, because when he got a team "broken in" well enough for an ordinary person to handle, he sold it and started breaking a new pair of broncs that only he could manage. Unfortunately, I didn't know all of this at the time, in fact I didn't really know where the "other place" was exactly. But that is understandable, since I was only two years old. Still, I trusted my grandfather, who was a strong and rugged farmer, with a love for life in his soul and a bit of mischief in his heart. That is, I trusted him until suddenly realizing he intended to kill the entire family by plunging horses, wagon and all of us into the Arkansas River.

As I began to scream and beg Pop not to do it, two of my teenaged aunts grabbed me and held me tightly between them, reassuring me with loving words and hugs. But it didn't help much because I thought I was a goner.

To this day I carry the vivid memories of the furious sound of horses and wagon plunging into that river, drowning out my screams of terror; the icy cold river water stinging my tearful cheeks, and the hugs and love of a family caring for and protecting me.

Then something wonderful happened—when I opened my eyes and realized I hadn't drowned. I looked forward and saw the majestic and powerful horses pulling the wagon through the water. They became a magical force taking us to safety and lifting us out of the river on the opposite bank.

I felt a little ashamed for being such a baby—which, in fact, is what I was. But nobody shamed me about it. Rather, they comforted me and quieted my fears. It was an extremely empowering experience because I realized for the first time that I was alive!

I am sure Pop was wrong about many things after that, but in that moment, he earned my trust forever. From my point of view, in those pre-World War II years, our's was a happy clan. If the adults had problems, the small children didn't hear much about it.

Mom's kitchen had a big wood-burning cook stove, and a hand water pump at the sink. She made fresh biscuits every morning, and fried potatoes and salty home-cured bacon. Her kitchen was a magical wonderland of comforting sights and smells and sounds. We drank water from a bucket with a metal dipper and raw skimmed milk from a big pitcher. The cream was taken off and sold at the market. The raw milk had a wild gamey taste that I hated. I didn't believe it when they told me I drank it as a baby. We heated water on the stove on Saturday night, so we could all take a bath in a wash tub. We bathed religiously, everyone, once a week, whether we needed it or not. The kitchen became the bathroom, where it was warm. The girls bathed first. The water was changed two or maybe three times. But by the time I had a turn, the water was always pretty murky looking. I couldn't complain because Pop always bathed last. We bathed with lye soap made from hog fat, soap that could take your hide off if it wasn't properly cured.

Wash day was Monday, with more lye soap and blueing and rinsing and wringing and hanging on a line. This time the soap was grated up so it would dissolve more easily.

We had horses and hogs and hounds, cats, milk cows, and chickens and dishware that came in an oatmeal box, and cars that came with a crank. If a chicken stopped laying, it was destined for the stew pot, and my mom could always tell—or so she said.

On Saturday we went to town. The kids got to go to the movies: Westerns with Gene, and Hoppy, Lash La Rue, and Captain Midnight serials to keep us coming back. We parked at Mack's (a gasoline station where Pop traded). Mom and the girls sold eggs and butter and used the money for shopping. Sometimes they went to Sweeny's Feed store to buy a flour sack, or sometimes just to look at prints for a future dress.

Everyone worked hard. We kids played hard and, when we tried to work, made messes. Mom and mud were constant adversaries. Mud was clever and relentless. It was constantly trying to sneak into the house on our clothes, and shoes and bodies. Mom keep a constant vigil and could battle it to a standstill. But if she doubted for one minute our resolve to her mudless cause, we could find ourselves in serious trouble.

My favorite place in the whole world was mom's sewing room with the well-used foot-powered Singer in the corner. The room was filled with scraps of this and pieces of that; old rags and worn out socks, cut into strips for hoop rugs in the making. There were work clothes in for mending, and knitting needles, and quilts half done, and dress patterns stuffed in shoe boxes. There were Sears, Robuck and Company catalogs patiently waiting for a one way trip to the outhouse. They seemed in no hurry.

There was a sunbeam that visited mom's sewing room in the morning and lit up a world of microscopic dust. It was a universe that I might never have noticed had the sunbeam not smiled through the window and pointed it out.

My older brother, cousin and I had a favorite game in Mom's sewing room. We would look through the old catalogs for pictures of pretty girls and try to be the first to kiss them. We especially liked ladies in their underwear. Since we thought this might be naughty, we did it only when no adults were close.

The nights in Colorado are cool and in winter can be bitterly cold. When it snowed—and we could talk Mom into it—we made ice cream with the snow.

It felt safe to go to bed with my brother and cousin and whoever else needed to share the space, on homemade feather tics, with coarse cotton sheets and homemade quilts stacked high. There were chamber pots to use in the middle of the night, if you could bear the cold.

There was a great and empowering ritual the men occasionally performed. At night, just before retiring, all the men would go together and pee from the rear porch. There, with my clan surrounding me, looking up at a clear cold Colorado starlit night, the mysteries of the universe dancing above me, may be the time when I was as close to Heaven as I have ever felt. The feeling was more than safe, I felt able. I felt ready. I felt whole.

I am sure this is a male ritual, as ancient as humankind or older. It may be about marking territory. When I asked myself more recently why we didn't do this great empowering ritual every night, I have concluded my grandmother didn't care much for how the territory smelled once we had marked it.

This was a great time for me to be born. I was surrounded by kinsmen who loved, valued, protected and empowered me.

But this is only where the story begins. Because when I was 5 years old, my mother, who had been missing from my life for sometime, came back to Colorado. She had a new husband and we moved to California to fight World War II. We moved into a small trailer, in a trailer park next to an army camp where our new stepfather was being trained how best to help preserve our freedom by killing people.

Before long I found myself huddled with my brother under the bed of the small trailer, in a "blackout," clutching a butcher knife. Our family and my mother, it seemed—had abandoned us and left us waiting for some Japs to break down the door and kill and eat us.

So I did the only thing I could do. I turned into a fat frog. I began to live my life as a metaphor, in a spell cast upon me by abandonment and fear. My father was gone. My family was gone. My mother, who loved me dearly, had never been there in the first place.

Now a little boy turned into a frog was not so noticeable to the humans looking from the outside, who were busy fighting wars. I was only 5 years old, so I had no conscious understanding of it at the time. Only looking back now can I begin to grasp the trauma my psyche went through. I wanted to disappear. I began sinking more and in the mud of fear and growing fat as an armor for self protection.

I felt worthless and unlovable because my clan had abandoned me. I was swallowed up by shame. I got lost in abandonment and I forgot who I was on a conscious level. I let the frog handle things.

A painful hole began to grow in my heart where the love and protection of my family clan had once dwelled. This was scary and I started trying to fill the hole with things. Food, which I began to fear we would not have enough of, because we were poor, became my first "filler" of choice. Food became my friend, my companion, my mother and father. It was a sedative that could, if not fill the hole, at least, ease my fear and pain.

As I grew older, the frog began thinking he could be human. But I was always there, at a subconscious level to let him know that he was only a fat frog, flawed at the core, that feared being exposed for pretending to be human.

When I was about 15 years old, I began to pretend I was an athlete and started playing football. Football was full of lessons. At my very core level, I always knew I was destined to fail because frogs, even fat frogs, don't have what it takes to succeed at much of anything. And if they go out on a limb, the risk and fear of exposure is always there.

Still, a football team can become a kind of a made-up family clan. And this was the best thing I had been exposed to since my days on my grandparents farm. I was fortunate that I had good fatherly coaches.

But the most important thing occurred on a sweltering day on the practice field not long after I had begun my football experience.

I was, at the time, a big, clumsy, immature crybaby frog. We were practicing a "two on one drill" and I had to take a turn as the defensive lineman. My two senior class men opponents were both "All City" caliber linemen. They began to soundly clean my plow, routing me, pushing me, back and knocking me on my can. But Coach Rose won't let it end there. He stopped all the other drills and let the entire team watch while he kept our confrontation going.

My coach must have seen some value there worth fighting for because—as the drill progressed, over countless turns, with Coach Rose urging and instructing and the entire team pulling for me—I began to stand my ground and win the battle. Then suddenly in the dust and mud and grime and blood on that hot September afternoon, fighting back the wall of exhaustion, with tears flowing from my eye, I became unblockable. I became unstoppable. I began to win; my team mates cheering me on.

That is when I felt the shift and I realized I could make it in the world by being strong and becoming fearless. I experienced a right of passage. It wasn't total transformation. I didn't become a human again (that would come later). But the fat frog died and I become a fearless bull frog.

Next I met a princess. She was being held captive by a wicked witch in an ivory tower. Being a young naive fearless bull frog, I thought I could pretend to be a white knight and rescue her from the wicked witch. I pretended so hard that for many years I actually thought I was a white knight.

She liked my fearlessness and being rescued from time to time. Yet she remained captive in her ivory tower. But we married anyway and tried to raise a family and live like "normal" humans. But this was not to be, because the wicked witch, although she pretended to accept me, would not remove the spell that she had cast over the princess' life. This was because the wicked witch's own life had long since vanished, and feared she would disappear too if she could not project herself through the princess.

We lived our lives in turmoil. I felt that I didn't deserve having such a beautiful and wonderful princess, since I was only a lowly bull frog. I spent enormous amounts of energy manipulating her, trying to control her, to keep her from discovering my webbed feet. I was continually battling the wicked witch for her release from the tower. Strangely, the princess appeared sometimes helpless and in desperate need of rescue, while at other times she seemed possessed by the witch and would run in panic from our relationship. The truth is that because of our childhood experience, we both feared the vulnerability required to obtain the intimacy for us or our relationship to become whole.

Later, not long after my transforming near-death experience had turned me back to being human, the once-suppressed poet in me wrote about the dynamics of our relationship, in many ways similar to the fairy tale Rapunsel, which I believe reflects the romantic paradox of western civilization.[1]

The princess and I carried on this tumultuous relationship for over a decade leading up to my transforming experience. Finally on my 30th birthday, July 29, 1967, after we had been married, divorced and remarried, my transformation experience took place.

It happened while I was living in southern Ohio, managing a construction project. A few months earlier she had left me for a second time. It happened with no discernible warning. I came home from work one day and she and our children had vanished.

---

1 Mr. Trask's NDE-inspired poem, "The Ivory Tower," and others are available by request via the publisher.

It was several days before I knew they were all right and several months before I found them and talked to them again.

I was devastated because not only had she abandoned me, but she had run in apparent fear and taken all that I held dear with her. I spent the next few months outwardly condemning her. But my subconscious knew she had discovered the worthless spell-bound frog that wasn't worthy of being loved.

Then came my day of transformation. I was getting ready to move to my next construction assignment, packing up our furniture and belongings when I discovered an old diary she had written when we first met in high school. I had always taken pride in the fact that I wasn't one to snoop into the inner privacy of others. Although I had seen the diary before, I had never seriously considered reading it. Yet, in my present state of anguish, reading it became irresistible.

I was looking for information to further indict her. I wanted to question her fidelity from the very beginning of our relationship. I wanted to expose her true intention (which I had convinced myself was to do the wicked witch's bidding by controlling, manipulating and misusing me while being unfaithful). I felt this might be the means by which I could free myself from the agony and anguish that were consuming me.

I was wrong. I found in the pages of that diary a princess who truly and passionately loved me, not for the frog I was, but rather for the man I could be. She had, at a deep level of understanding, found the little abandoned boy hiding under the bed of that small trailer in California. He had remained there transfixed, without a family, unable to grow to manhood. Lo and behold, she had been attempting to rescue me, while I was trying to rescue her.

Suddenly, I was caught by the irony of this enigma. I had spent what seemed like forever, trying to hide from her that I was a worthless toad, and all along she had reached past that and sensed the real human locked in this metaphor—this spell. I became consumed by grief for the hell we had been through, and now. But even more for fear that I had lost her. In an instant, I realized that all the controlling macho, bullfrog being John Wayne things I had been taught and tried to believe in were bullshit. My ego was killed, crushed by the weight of the truth.

Then the most wonderful event in my life happened. My ego had been blocking my channels to Creation. With my ego crushed the channels were opened wide. An angel from the cosmos swooped down and kissed the enchanted frog on the lips, and I was once again transformed into a human. The mood became sublime. Time stood still. Eternity was in full view before me. I felt the presence of my Creator and was flooded with knowing.

In a sudden crescendo, all the mysteries of the universe came rushing by me. In that instant, I knew all there was to know. The information swirled all around me, then suddenly rose up. Like glass, it seemed to shatter and come crashing down around me. It all seemed to be traveling at light speed, so I didn't receive much information with this initial blast except I was forever altered and I knew—I had always known at a spiritual level—the whole truth (which was now lying there shattered and fragmented at my feet, ready to be retrieved).

I was dancing with life and tears of joy, and tears of melancholy. Then a poet emerged from my depth and I was astounded, because before this psychic shift, the only writing I had ever been serious about was a good business letter. He kept me awake for two days while he composed my very first poem, a poem about the relationship I have been describing.[2]

I still carry a great many warts left over from being a frog; and although the witch is now dead, in many ways, she lives on in the princess' head. But we both have since realized the truer dynamics of this fairy tale and are healing ourselves.

I have spent the last 28 years since my transforming event growing in enlightenment and attempting to put together the pieces that were shown to me that memorable day, pieces that show how we are connected to the universe, our Creator and each other, in some cohesive way that might lend clarity to me, and be of benefit to others.

I have since come to realize that the whole truth can never be unveiled by a single human; that my best hope is to stay focused on my path of truth. It is a path without a finish line. I also know that I am not alone, although my event took place years before

---

2 "Love and Money."

the "New Age" movement became widely recognized. This Creator Force is all around us. It speaks to us all in slightly different ways. If we can listen with our hearts and learn, we can each bring our own unique piece to the puzzle.

I know with my heart: humanity is about to issue forth with a new evolved human paradigm. It may seem a little scary now. But it is going to be wonderful.

*Richard Trask*

*The poems mentioned in his article can be purchased for three dollars by sending check or money order with a stamped, self-addressed envelope to Richard Trask, 1304 Langham Creek, Suite 498, Houston, Texas 77084.*

# ᴳod Beckoned & I Backed Away

*Edward lives in Austin, Texas where he provides counseling, care and guidance in matters of grief, death and dying. Operating as Compassionate Personal Care, he facilitated individuals, families and groups in embracing death and making one's own final arrangements. He is a cofounder of the Austin chapter of IANDS and is active in promoting healthy death awareness.*

Howdy. My name is Edward Salisbury and I'm a survivor of multiple near-death experiences. I'd like to tell you what it was like, what happened and what it is like now.

In December of 1969, I was, in most eyes, a rising star. I was a young, white male in a free America. I was going for the good life. You might say I was a product of the Madison Avenue/Hollywood hype. I was the firstborn of three children of a middle American couple. I became very athletic and was supposedly intelligent. In fact, I was invited to join a Mensa group but I turned it down because all the women were too tall. I played rugby and weighed 210 pounds. I was out to grab all the gusto I could. I remember affirming to myself that I was free, white, good-looking and deserved it all.

I was brought up as a good Episcopalian, an altar boy and Boy Scout. As I approached graduation from high school, I had a big debate: do I want the seminary or the military? After all, both wore tight collars. I chose the military and went to the U. S. Naval Academy in Annapolis, Maryland. For the first year I felt oppressed, challenged and occasionally rewarded. Desiring to quit, I deferred to my father's wishes and went back for a second year to win top honors. But there was a real seeking within that led me to resign and finish college at Texas A&M University in logic and physics.

My beliefs were built around a Father in God but I didn't know how to get in touch with or find God. I'd gone from the traditional strong belief to strong doubt by the time I was working in Atlanta two years out of college. Working for a major corporation as an information liaison specialist, representing the computer division to other corporate subsidiaries and executive offices, I was on the fast track. I wanted to "grab all the gusto" that I could, as fast as I could. I believed if I worked long enough, hard enough and made love to enough women, I would have the good life.

I say love. I didn't know what it was. For me, it was that tender feeling when someone held you and occasionally that glorious feeling of sharing a climax. That's all I knew about it. Then came the wreck December 30, 1969.

That evening, I went to a football game—the Bluebonnet Bowl, Georgia Tech—with some friends, enjoying a nice evening of chanting, raving and partying. As I was driving home on a winding city street, a car swerved down the street. I swerved to avoid getting hit and the right tire of my Firebird convertible caught the curb. I heard a loud BANG—I'd crashed into a tree. I was catapulted into and through the tree. It felt like going up an elevator in a tall building. Going down through the veins of the tree, I popped out at the top, looked down on the yard below and saw my car. There was smoke coming from under the hood, people running out of the house next to it. As I looked closely, I saw this body slumped on the steering wheel. For a moment, I looked in awe as I recognized it AS MY BODY! If that is my body, then who am I?

No sooner had I grasped that I was not my body than I found myself swooped up like dust in a vacuum hose. I was catapulted into a different experience. I traveled through a dark tunnel like a spaceship through stars. The experience was breathtaking—the silence beautiful. In the faint distance was the tiniest hint of beautiful music, music beyond anything I've heard on earth.

For a brief moment, I fixed on a tiny light in the distance. The light seemed to get a little brighter and a little brighter as I came closer until in a moment I found myself immersed—flooded—in the bright brilliant white beautiful light. You know when you come out of a dark movie theater in the middle of the day, the light is everywhere? Well, this is what it was like, but not oppressive. It was embracing, nourishing.

If you can remember a time when you had been chilled to the bone—that cold, wet, shivering feeling when you couldn't wait to get home to get out of the freezing cold, wet clothes and then when you immerse yourself into a warm, hot bathtub full of water, you can just glimpse what it was like to be immersed in a warm, loving, nourishing, graceful, glorious light—euphoric ecstasy. You would have take all the miraculous, wondrous, joyous, glorious experiences of being well-fed, loved, cosmic orgasm bundled together for an inkling of what it was like to be embraced by the light of God. That presence, beauty and joy awakened me like a cold shower in the morning. I came to in a way that I'd never been awakened before. In the vast light and beautiful surroundings, I felt totally at peace—calm, enchanted and loved. It wasn't love as we believe it but love as all-knowing, an essence of cosmic consciousness.

In wanting to know anything and being able to find the answer for any question I had—I had only to think about it and I could turn and look to know the answer. Why I was born into the family I was? What is the purpose of America? Who is God? All that is known to all of us—when we are embraced by the light of God.

After awhile (time stood still), I could feel beings of light all around me. As I focused and looked at this collection of beings, one came forward. This angel of light, as it got closer, became clearer. There, standing before me, reaching out his right hand, beckoning me to come, was the Jesus that I had prayed to as a child, that I had served as an altar boy, and that I had doubted as a young graduate. This being stood there before me, reaching out with a grin, a smile, a countenance of total glory and grace. His eyes poured love, glorious, powerful love, into my being. With his left hand, he pointed up and behind him. I received telepathically that I was being directed to look beyond him. But to take my eyes off this beautiful, wonderful love being was hard to do, yet it was a direction, a loving commandment.

As I obeyed, I saw an even more glorious person, a being, there, sitting up on a platform, in a chair or throne. This precious, beautiful man radiated glory—with a wonderful flowing white beard, a fantastic smile and glorious, loving eyes. There was this Santa Claus-like grandfather. Godfather-like, Father God himself, he was looking into my eyes, waving with his right hand to come. He commanded and beckoned me to come as he patted his left knee.

For the first time in all this experience, I became self-aware. I wasn't caught up with what was in front of me or what was happening to me. I became conscious of myself. You know how a child, when his turn comes to sit on Santa's lap, sometimes recoils? Well, that was me. God beckoned and I backed away.

I thought, "Who? Me? You want me?" I doubted him. In the next instant, I was teleported to his lap. His arm was wrapped around my back, his beautiful smile and glorious loving face were pouring out wonderful, beautiful, delicious, delightful, empowering and UNCONDITIONAL LOVE. I was in his lap and he was filling me with the grace and glory and joy of Heaven. The message came to me: "This is where you always are in truth." God then pointed down to his feet and asked, "Are you through?"

I found it hard to pull my eyes from his beautiful face. Again it was a direction, a commandment to look and answer. Am I through? I looked to where he pointed. There arrayed like toys on a floor (or tv sets) were visions of my life. It was what I have come to know as a life review.

I focused and looked closely. Ah, it was a memory. In the next moment as I focused on one image, I was reexperiencing when I was four or five years old stealing Coke bottles from my neighbor's garage! This was more than just a glimpsing memory. I relived it! In the middle of the dark, mildewy garage, I could smell the room. I could feel the temperature. I heard the clinking of the bottles under my shirt, as I went running down the alley thinking, "Nobody will ever know!"

As I completed the recall, this re-experience, I realized that here I am in the lap of God and boy, WAS I ASHAMED! I turned to God and said, "Uh-oh. I'm sorry, that was bad!" God grinned and said. "It is neither bad nor good. It is something you have done. Are you through?"

That was a shock. It took a few moments to really "grok" that concept, that truth. I was directed again to these images with the question, "Are you through?"

I relived the teasing of young girls, deformed with a cleft palate as I mocked her. I got to feel how she felt. I felt the pain, the shame, the remorse and I got to feel her wishing she was dead. Returning, I told God that was bad. He gave the same response with unconditional love. "It is a lesson to be learned. Are you through?"

Turning to God, in pride I thought, "That's good, isn't it?" The answer was the same. I relived the saving of a girl from drowning, in high school. Trough every memory I had, through shame, fear, pride, wit, greed, ego, fantasies, the answer was: Life is a lesson.

There is no way I wanted to go back to the world living with blinders on, into the physical limitations. Am I through? Yes. I'm through! Only, I want to make sure mom knows I'm okay. I reached out from God's lap to close the book that lay at God's feet and be free of earthly attachments.

I came to in Grady Memorial Hospital in Atlanta, Georgia, with my mother at my feet, three weeks later. I was delivered by the ambulance to the hospital d.o.a. My body had been crushed, my scalp broken open, my chin hanging on my flailed chest, my ribs collapsed against my backbone, my intestines ruptured.

Later, I asked the physician, "When you have gunshots, burns, bruises, suffering patients and you also have this bag full of bones d.o.a., you usually don't spend time on lost causes."

He grinned and chuckled, insisting that I never repeat this. That evening there was a young intern on duty—business was slow—and he gave my body to him as an academic exercise, challenging him to bring back any vital signs. So I'm living testimony to the value of academic exercises.

Obviously, the intern was able to revive some vital signs. The crash team jumped in and put me back together. In the following five years, I underwent seven major surgeries with recurring abscess infections as a result of the ruptured intestines. The last one was for a collapsed lung arising from my drowning. But that's another story.

As I attempted to explain my experience to the physicians who cared for me in the many weeks and months following, I was confronted with doubt and denial. The experience was profound and undeniable, yet as I tried to explain bits and pieces of it as they became clear in my memory, I was told (very gently but firmly), "You are hallucinating. Drugs and trauma can do things like that. I wouldn't talk about it if I were you. They're liable to think you're crazy, mentally unstable."

Well, in the many years since, I've come to understand the medical profession is not equipped to understand or assist in the process of reintegrating the profound spiritual experience of the NDE into living day-to-day life. The most significant effect of the near-death experience on my life was the loss of fear of death. I realized there is nothing to fear in death. Actually, it is a gift, a transformation into a form of spiritual being without the fetters or restrictions of physical life. Second—a quest for knowledge, having been exposed to conscious cosmic universal knowledge, the book of truth and spiritual knowing. Having experienced total love, unconditionally, I am transformed in ways I still struggle to comprehend and express it. It is the ability to love each and every human being as an expression of God, knowing that we are spiritual beings having a human experience, not human beings having spiritual experiences, that inspires me today.

Beyond universal love is the driving force to do service. We serve as counselors, caregivers, doctors, nurses, ministers, therapists, healers in many ways. Also, many of us become quite psychic. I express it as "spiritually attuned," getting to be more sensitive to an individual's love and hate, fear and hope. We are gifted with expanded sensory awareness. The quest for knowledge still drives me to read, study, listen, learn, share with every subject, from eastern mysticism, western spiritual and universal philosophies. I've been a student of yoga, a minister of healing arts (native American healings), and a student of other people's experiences. I've learned the universal love is that unconditional beauty in every being. Now, this can be a real challenge. Just by knowing it doesn't mean others will understand it.

What is important, really? The service angle—what is it all about? It's not the things you have or places you have been, nor the monuments, books, reputations you've created. What makes the difference is the cumulative results of the service you've given to others. How compassionate have you been to others? That experience of knowing how the little girl felt when I ridiculed her, the pain I created in her, is a flagpole or warning sign of how important it is to treat everyone as we would want to be treated, with respect, appreciation and even love.

Following the accident in Atlanta, I tried to return to work as a computer guru. I found myself unfulfilled. I began searching for that love in the church. I returned as an active member of the church community but I also reached out, studying other teachings and mystical groups like the Association of Research and Enlightenment, based on Edgar Cayce. I married the woman I had been dating. I began new studies, in business and law, later schools of education, communication and more. I had also been working on the side in real estate during Austin's big real estate boom in the early 70's and had made more money in one summer than in all the previous twenty years of my life put together.

My wife and I decided to start a family. Being unable to conceive (because of my many surgeries), we moved to Houston where I could get a "regular" job in hopes of adopting children. I found a job as an executive account rep, a wheeler-dealer in computer service with all the trademarks of a successful life.

We enjoyed the good life. One October evening, we borrowed my sister's fourteen foot sailboat to go to Corpus Christi to camp out. Coming back, the boom swung and hit her in the head, knocking her overboard, drowning her.

I was devastated. While I had no fear of death for myself, I was angry at Gloria's death. How could God let this happen? Yet I knew God's only will is for us to know, experience and express unconditional love. It wasn't God's work—it was one of life's experiences.

In the following months, I became disillusioned in my success with the computer world. My partner, my lover and my friend was gone. My purpose and direction were empty. I began to travel. I experienced another near-death experience (that is another story, too) and have now committed my life to service.

Lessons I've learned from the near-death experiences:

*God is unconditional love, ever-present, all-powerful and beyond our ability to understand. We are vessels of that grace, that force. We are instruments of God with the ability to express or deny that force and power as we see fit.*

*God's will for us is to know, experience and express unconditional love in everything we do.*

*To the degree I can get myself out of the way—my self-centered fear, ego, greed, doubt—God will express Himself/herself through me.*

*God is like water. Our beliefs are like cups. God will fill our vessel, whatever the shape.*

*We never die.*

*God blesses us all.*

Your brother,

*Edward, The Phoenix*

# We Will Live Forever

*Gerry Cosme works as a contractor in Houston.*

Place: Beaumont, Texas....Houston.

Time: May, 1978.

Hello out there. world. My name is Gerry Cosme and back in May 1978 over Memorial Day weekend I had an experience that was life-altering! I was a passenger in a little car that was broadsided by a college student who ran a four-way stop sign (he was D.W.I.) and hit us and punched my lights out.

I was killed in that car accident. The paramedics revived me on the way to the hospital and kept me stabilized there. While this was going on I was going through a spiritual transition; I didn't realize it at the time. It was peaceful as I traveled through my life (my higher self toward God's world while my physical body went through four months of intensive care and four hospitals). Eleven months later I started to function somewhat as a human being again. I had to relearn all about myself. For two to four years it was like being a child. My wife couldn't handle the emotional part (she wasn't strong enough) so she decided to leave and said her good-byes because I wasn't the same person she married. I guess not, after telling my team of doctors at Methodist Hospital that I encountered God while traveling through an off-white peaceful tunnel to my maker. No wonder people thought I acted strange and did things differently— so did my good friends around me. Not until three or four years later while I was reading a book that Dr. Raymond Moody had written about people who came to him and told him of their experiences did I realize that I too had gone through a similar event. Ever since that wild weekend, I feel peace and love toward other people, a feeling that still astounds me. Yet I still sleep good at night by the grace of God. But while I sleep I still wander off.

I've always been a God-fearing person. I've always had strong feelings about my faith in God and Jesus Christ our coming King and Savior. As a Christian I've always been different and done things a little differently than most people—that is how I explain the way I am today.

My life has changed in dramatic ways: while I was going through my round trip in my tunnel I was recycled a lot by a higher force and thrown back to Earth. As I was unconscious, I mentally saw visions of spirits walking past me through a wall in Grand Central Park. I was welcomed by God and Jesus who returned me to Earth back in November of 1978. They told me I was not finished with my journey through life. As in *Luke 12:22, 23*, Jesus said unto his disciples:

*"Therefore I say to you take no thought for your life, what you should eat neither for the body what ye shall put on. The life is more than meat and the body is more than raiment."*

The spirit of consciousness is the inspired message of the scriptures. Thus your consciousness becomes the law of supply and you producing its own image and likeness in the form of all those things necessary to your well-being.

We should begin our day with the inner reminder of our true identity. We must identify ourselves as spirits, as principles, as the law of life in our affairs—that point of God's consciousness—by using the identity of good pouring through us the same as it poured through Jesus our coming King and Creator.

We go out into life as the presence of God. Because we are the law of love, we are the light of the world—you must realize yourself to be life, truth and love. We must accept "Jesus Christ" revelation of the *I am* as an ascended master until it becomes realization with you. We are never outside the presence of God's being. We should seek and find the kingdom within. We should see each other as traveling on the path of light. We should cultivate the consciousness of the presence of God every moment.

Since then I experience a lot of better and bigger things in life as long as I don't forget what Jesus says in the New Testament of the Bible: "...and I say to you love your neighbor as yourself"—the llth commandment. He gave it to us while he was prophesying in Jerusalem and teaching society about what he experienced. To this day I still am energized and see the light (the spirit of God). I call it every so often when I'm going through one of my spiritual encounters in life. In my opinion I feel that God, my father, was trying to show me what Heaven would be like if I continue my way of loving my neighbor as myself during my physical lifetime here on Earth. Since I have experienced death, the dying process (I was considered clinically dead), I now realize we will live forever "spiritual" as Jesus Christ was (our coming King and Savior) when he rose from the dead and returned to Earth in a glorified body. There is a spiritual existence after our physical death.

May God bless you all. Respectfully submitted,

*Mr. Gerald J. Cosme, God's Child*

# osmic Joke

*Porfirio (Phil) Acosta's near-death experience and the years of therapy and healing that followed gave birth to a series of children's stories. These stories contain no violence or criticism and stress the natural perfection in the creation of the child. Elsie The Raindrop and the dozens of other characters in the Raindrop series fit naturally into the needs of children everywhere and of all ages.*

After five years of intense training in the areas of weight training, swimming and cycling, I decided to relocate to Houston to pursue my dream of a Triathlon in the Olympics. My goals were unknown to my family. I had taken a loan out on my father's signature to pursue my dreams.

Upon arriving in Houston, I took the first job offered (in a warehouse) in order to make my first payment due on the first of the month. Everything was going just fine until one day—about lunch time—I was assigned the task of relocating some furniture to the second floor. Though alone, I found the task effortless because of my physical condition.

With all the furniture in the center of the room, I looked at my accomplishment proudly, knowing that the task easily required two persons. Without warning, the room started to rumble and sway. Because of my experiences with earthquakes in California, all that my mind could comprehend was that an earthquake was shaking the building.

Seconds later, I found myself eye-to-eye with the second floor's baseboard and my arms stretched out above me. Free-falling into the room downstairs, I landed on the corner of a desk with my tail bone taking all the impact. The furniture above, trailing me by seconds, severely compressed my spine. In other words, I had been crushed between the two floors. The years of competition training had paid off in a way I had never expected—otherwise I could have been paralyzed or suffocated by all the furniture on top of me.

I must have lost consciousness for a while as I remember all the dust had settled. The best way I can describe the pain that awoke me is as follows:

Have you ever struck your funny bone? Remember what that lighting-like sharp pain shooting down your arm felt like? Well, that is the sensation that I felt in my entire body. I also had a severe head concussion and whiplash.

I remember being wheeled into the emergency room as I went into convulsions brought on by the burning fiery pain. I remember an angel, a nurse by the name of Barbara Henderson. She was present as I was placed on the gurney. There happened to be an enormous security guard on hand helping to wheel me into the emergency room. By then I was consumed, exploding into a fireball of pain.

Then, before the triage team could respond, I fell deep, deep within myself. I had fallen into a distance far beyond the physical, I was dead in the center, the eye of the storm. I can describe it as though I was gazing out through two distant peepholes in my head. I no longer felt any pain. All was peaceful, all was calm. I was at peace.

I remember watching the emergency team executing their roles, moving rapidly doing this and that. I remember hearing the security guard stating his observation, "I think he's on Angel Dust." Nurse Barbara Henderson's response was to tell them to shut up and secure my arms so I could be strapped down on the gurney. This large man then grabbed both my arms, leaned on me with all his weight. At that time I heard myself say to myself, "I am going to lie to these people."

Within a fraction of a second, I found myself shooting into this darkness, a darkness full of micro dots of sparkling pink, blue and white lights. I traveled forward in an arc from left to right. I existed only as a thought, a thought which I now describe and understand as God's thought.

I repeatedly glanced left and right. I was aware of the directions. How I knew I was turning left and right I do not know as there was no physical reference to left and right, but it was just understood.

*Ecclesiastes 9:5* states "The living are conscious that they will die; but as for the dead, they are conscious of nothing at all." I find this to be true because as soon as I entered the darkness, I had no awareness or memory of my life, my dreams, my pain nor my loved ones. No anger, hate just a different consciousness. In crossing over, I did die, but I did not cease to exist: the process only altered my point of perception and awareness. I recall the thoughts of a wise man, "You cannot create or destroy energy, you can only change it."

By the time I turned my awareness to the left, I came upon a donut-shaped white cloud that transcended all that was before me. I had no physical body; I could not hear the power that the swirling cumulus cloud of light possessed. I can best describe it as standing at the base of Niagara Falls. The cloud swirled from within to without. The cloud was so white and pure that it glowed blue with traces of pink.

I never had any fear at all and I felt a bit like a foreigner but at the same time I felt like a homesick pilgrim who had ventured out to see the new world and had returned back home to his family. A bit like when I went back home to El Paso after a 10-year absence. I sort of knew my way around but since there had been so much change and growth, I was a bit lost and occasionally need assistance with directions.

After gazing at the cloud I then proceeded to continue forward only to bounce off an invisible door. I bounced off the door on my three attempts to go through. On the third attempt, I just floated there, hovering with a slight up and down pattern. I then looked deep into the center of the cloud only to see millions of entities just being there. I can describe them as follows.

Have you ever tried to put a point on a dull lead pencil? Remember the smudge left on the paper after you rubbed the pencil tip to a sharp point? That is what I saw. Sort of a bunch of smudges. I believe that this was eternity—free of time and space—because the smudges a million miles to the back were the same size as the ones in the front. No vanishing point. There were no levels to refer to as floors, but there were some higher than others and some lower than others, yet without reference as to above and below, or back or front. In a way I knew them all and they knew me, a warm and loving reception.

As I tried once more to enter with denial, a face approached me out from the left in an arc. The face had all the human features such as eyes ears and a nose but no hair. The face represented two things that I grew up to respect as a child: age and wisdom. I knew that the face was masculine in gender and represented great authority. As the face floated before me with a presence of great authority, I was given one and only one message by mental telepathy: "YOU ARE NOT ALONE."

The face then departed following the same arc as it arrived. Then from the right, the very same face approached me following the exact opposite path except this time I knew the face was feminine. Once again the face represented great authority and she only had one message for me: "YOU ARE NOT ALONE." The face then departed in the same fashion as it had arrived.

I tried once more to enter but this time, as I bounced off the invisible door, I felt myself start to fall back. I resisted and fought but as I existed only as a thought, I had nothing to hold on to. Nothing to hold on with. I felt myself fall back at an incredible speed and force.

I remember the bounce I felt when I hit my body. I can describe it as the thud a parachutist might experience hitting the ground after his chute failed to open. I heard someone (and I believe it was nurse Barbara Henderson) shout, "He's back!" Then I lost consciousness.

I do not remember the length of time that followed. When a team of about eight doctors came to visit me, they inquired about all the questions I was asking about my experiences. They listened quietly without comments. They said thank you and then they pulled the green curtain back around and I heard one of the student doctors say, "Wow! Did you hear that shit!" as if I could not hear them past the green fabric.

Since then, I have seen the world, events, fellow brothers and sisters with different eyes, probably nonphysical eyes. I also find it very difficult to fit in this world as it is: cruel, selfish and corrupt. Someone is aware of all there is.

I also remember an experience my mother shared with me when I went home several years later. She told me about a time when she was getting lunch ready for my little brother who was at school when all of a sudden she felt very sleepy and told my little sister to finish lunch as she needed to lie down. She had a daydream in which she saw me drowning. Knowing that I used to like to surf—a hobby I picked up in California—she thought she saw me drowning but in fact she saw me falling through the air. My mother, as all mothers, has a spiritual connection with her children that has no bounds. As for the "I'm going to lie to these people..."

The lie was a COSMIC JOKE. The joke is our misunderstanding of the liberation we mourn as DEATH.

*Porfirio Acosta*

# Resurrection

*Billy Spellman now lives peacefully in the countryside. He has a 22 year-old son and an 18 year-old daughter.*

My experience began in July of 1987. I was facing a divorce that I did not want. I considered a divorce the worst thing that could happen to anyone so I made a decision to die rather than be divorced. I had put a loaded and cocked gun to my head on several occasions but for some reason I still cannot explain to this day, I could not pull the trigger.

After going through these times with the gun, I decided to kill myself with drugs.

During and prior to these times with the gun, I had taken Darvocett N-100 tablets for occasional migraines. The doctor prescribed one or two for pain. It had been my experience that for my worst headache I could only take 1½ tablets at the most as two full tablets made me sick. Also, because of the fighting with my ex-wife prior to the divorce, I had from time to time taken Valium for anxiety. Two or three of the Valiums would put me to sleep for hours so I figured that if I were to take 100 Darvocett N-100's and 90 10 mg. Valium, it would for sure do the job of killing me. I got myself together 100 Darvocet N-100's and 90 10 mg. Valiums, got on my knees and prayed to God to forgive me for not being strong enough to face a divorce, poured several glasses of water, sat down in the easy chair and took all of the drugs. It was Tuesday morning around 7:30 a.m.

The next thing I remember was being in my bed and lifting my head off the pillows to see my sister and my ex-wife standing at the foot of my bed. After this, the next thing I remember was finding myself alive and awake in bed the following Friday evening.

I was able to talk to my sister after waking up that Friday evening and she was able to recall what day and time she had come by on her way to a doctor's appointment. She had come by at 7:45 a.m. that Tuesday morning about 15 minutes after I had taken the drugs. At the time of this writing, my sister now claims that she has no memory of those 3½ days.

My ex-wife has since the experience refused to talk to me about her most recent claim that she has no memory of anything prior to the December 1987 divorce.

I took massive doses of drugs, much more than enough to kill me.

The first thought after waking up that Friday evening was "What had gone wrong?" I was in total shock about being alive. I searched the bed and path to my easy chair for signs of passing any body fluids. I found nothing. I had somehow after taking the drugs made my way to the bed and stayed there without passing any fluids or solids for 3½ days. I have since calculated that I cannot take one dose such as the number of drugs divided by 3½ days without getting sick. After thinking about this and other spiritual experiences that I have had over the past eight years, I believe that God resurrected me from the dead.

After getting my bearings and deciding what to do next, I went to work on my next scheduled shift. I had been on a week-long vacation. Going around other people, I received another shock. I began to see what I call people's spirits.

The last thing I had done prior to taking the drugs was to get on my knees and pray to God to forgive me for not being strong enough to face a divorce. So I began to study the Bible in an effort to understand what was happening to me. I read everything I could get my hands on about death. And I began attending a near-death experience support group in Houston, Texas.

*Billy Spellman*

# Near (Eternal) Life Experience

*Bill Bingham received a BS in mechanical engineering from Rutgers, worked both as an engineer and a supervisor, taught college and had a business as an independent manufacturers' rep. He retired at age 47, successful. He studied human spirituality since his experience in 1962. He now shepherds a near-death experience support group in Houston, Texas and supervised this book project.*

At the time of my experience, I was agnostic.

I had a scientific education and seemed to be analytical by nature—more than a little left-brained. My parents, who were probably better true Christians than 99% of the people going to church, didn't attend church. They were very loving, caring parents with an excellent marriage. So, as a child, they would send me off on Sunday mornings with different neighbors so I could decide for myself. One week I might be a Presbyterian, another week a Methodist, another an Episcopalian, Baptist, Catholic etc.

None of this really felt quite right to me, though, and I quit going by mid-teens. My experience changed all of that. It came about as a result of emotional trauma: a big fight and splitting up with my wife. I loved this woman but I also knew at a deep level that she was not good for me. We fought a lot and I couldn't figure out why at the time. The night of the separation fight, I was torn by conflicting emotions; I wanted to go get her and bring her back but I knew it would just be more pain. So, I picked up a book, forced myself to sit down in bed and read, trying to get her off my mind. I could barely see the words I was so wrought up. But I forced myself to read one word at a time. I was constantly skipping back to read words or sentences over because thought of her interrupted my understanding. Eventually I fell asleep.

When I awoke, I picked up the book and started again one word at a time. There was divine order in the timing. I was teaching in college and we were just starting the semester break when the fight erupted, so I had two weeks off. I spent that time wrestling with my mind and emotions. The forced reading went on for several days before I began to experience some peace. A few more days and a deep peace had settled in. I decided to stay with it and kept reading.

Years later, when I was heavy into the practice of Zen Buddhism, I realized that I had become very one-pointed through the forced reading. This is a state that Zen strives mightily for.

Then one day as I was walking very peacefully from the kitchen into the living room, the top of my head blew off. I felt as though a river of light and glorious emotion was racing down through me with the force of a fire hose. It knocked me down. I laid on the floor in total awe. For several minutes the brain did not think, the body did not move. I could only experience the amazing feeling and light flowing through me. It is impossible to exaggerate the intensity of the feeling. One experiencer said "If you bring together every orgasm you ever had and every other feeling of love consummated and had them all happen to you at once—this will give you some idea." For me, it changed entirely my understanding of what the body and mind are capable of; virtually of what the mind and body are.

After several minutes of the light and outrageously glorious feeling, my being began to settle down to a state of extreme bliss. Then I started to see the history of my life go by. My emotional state now was one of unconditional love. The love was coming not only from me towards me but from everywhere. The room (probably the universe) was filled with love. My mental set was, "This life had been exactly the way it was supposed to be!" Supposed by who or what I didn't know. Again, the brain wasn't thinking this. The mind just knew it. It was as if it were placed there by some external power. Someone might look at that and say there is a plan for the universe or all creation or something. I certainly know there must be some plan for my life with all of its ups and downs, success and failures, or how would it be as it was "supposed" to be.

After that I started to see magnificent displays of knowledge. I had "understanding" of things in ways that we just don't possess in our everyday lives. That's why it is so very hard to describe these episodes. I'll just say that whatever I focused my mind on, I had complete knowledge of—I knew its molecular structure, its electrical and chemical structure, its complete design, the history of its existence, its place in the universe, etc., etc. Again, I did not calculate or think these things—they just sort of showed up in my mind without me asking or wishing for or expecting them.

Then I felt a slight physical jolt. My attention moved around inside myself to see what that was. Immediately I <u>knew</u> that all fear of death had just left. Now, I wasn't aware that I had much fear of death going into this whole experience, but I sure knew when it left.

At this point what felt like my first self-generated thought arose. The thought was "Well, I guess I can die now." It was as though this complete experience was what I was placed on this earth for and now I could leave, so I sort of looked around to see my death coming. It didn't seem to be about to show up.

The next thought that arose was "Well, I guess the rest is gravy." For 5 or 6 months after, it did look as though it was all going to be gravy; I was in a state of bliss day and night. One time, months later, I was just sitting there enjoying my bliss when even higher feelings started to roll over me. I started to see faces going by—people I knew—some well, some not so well. Again, the only state possible was awe. Shortly brain said "Wow. What's this? What's this? What's this?...! After a little while, a word appeared in consciousness The word was <u>forgiveness</u>. Apparently I had forgiven all those people. Many I didn't even know I had blamed for anything. Some weeks or months later another similar experience showed up. This time the word was <u>acceptance</u>. These two loving habits are bottom line principles in *A Course In Miracles*. Thirteen years later, the course was published. Nineteen years later I discovered it. The forgiveness, acceptance and ego-death experience I had then and later in Zen allowed me to know *A Course In Miracles* was—at the least—inspired writing. *A Course In Miracles* deals with ego alot.

It hasn't exactly been all gravy in the many years since my experience, though I have been blessed many, many times; though money meant much less to me after my experience. Though my religiosity did not improve my interest in the spiritual life exploded and I have spent much more time in church and temple, principally the Unity Church of Christianity (high on positive healthy thought and the Christ within and low on sin, guilt and false idols without) and Zen Buddhism (big on experiential practice and little on words). Even the rough spots haven't seemed so rough. They all turned out to be good learning experiences.

I call my experience a **mystical conversion experience**. Certainly I had contact with a higher consciousness or power. Certainly I was converted. I had—and I have—no doubt that there is a higher consciousness, that life is eternal at least in consciousness, and that death is nothing to be afraid of.

*Bill Bingham*

# The Dawning

*Due to a series of miraculous events, Claire now shares a song, "Mary's Lull-aby," sent by Mother Mary, and is available on tape. She also gives talks "bringing messages and hope for the people."*

The day before Thanksgiving of 1992, my husband and I were visiting his family for the holiday in Alton, Illinois. We decided to go to breakfast to a cute little place in Grafton which wasn't too far. As I looked out into the Mississippi river just feet away, I got a very intense feeling not easy to describe. I've had this feeling before that seems to have started coming only a year before that—a knowingness of great change, not just for my own life, but the lives of everyone on the planet, and the planet her-self. As this feeling swelled up inside of me, I couldn't hold myself back from the words that moved through my lips: "This river is going to flood like you've never seen it flood before." My brother-in-law said the river floods every year and never gets past the bank.

"This whole area is going to be under water," I said. He told me how impossible that was as we made our way to the restau-rant. After the holiday was over, we all got our hugs, said our good-byes and packed up the car for a long 15 hour drive home to Houston, Texas. I had been suffering from chronic back pain due mostly to a car accident and felt the increasing pressure from long hours of sitting in the car with only two or three quick bath-room and dinner stops. By the time we got home, we were exhausted and I was in severe pain. I had hoped that after a good nights sleep and stretching my body out, I would have some relief in the morning. As I awoke, I became aware that the sharp stabbing pains had not subsided but seemed to have amplified. The pain was so unbearable that I could hardly move any part of my body. My husband was still asleep and all I could do was pray. I asked God to bring me healing—instantly I felt a surge of energy shoot through my body from the top of my head down through my spine and down my legs to my toes. This energy brought my body from a curled-up position to a totally straight position all on its own as it shot through.

The next thing I knew, I was floating up to the ceiling fan above my bed and I realized I was no longer in my body. Then I was in a new place where there were the most beautiful iridescent geometric shapes, like bubbles, glowing. I was mesmerized by them and instinctively reached out my hands and pulled them inside me. As they moved in and through me, I was in total bliss. Somehow I knew that these shapes contained the wisdom and love of the universe.

Then I was soaring at a great speed through a tunnel. The tunnel looked alive, a living organism with colors, mostly pastels, not something that looked like it was built or made out of any man-made substance. It seemed to be lit up by something traveling with me because the light moved as I did. I'm still not sure because I could not see myself, but it was as if the light was coming from me. I was instantly back at that place where the iridescent beautiful geometric shapes were and I again reached for them and pulled them into me, experiencing the same bliss I did before. Then back in the tunnel again, as I was soaring through, I remember hearing myself saying, "I want to go, I want to go." With huge excitement about where I was going but no conscious knowledge as to where that was, I continued with "I want to go" as if I were a kid headed to Disneyland. Then I could see this incredible light ahead. One last time I said, "I want to—only if it is your will Father."

As I approached the end of the tunnel, there was an explosion of light, almost like watching a star explode. Then the next thing I remember, I was back in my body. "What was that?" I thought. I turned my head to look at my husband.

He opened his eyes and said, "Do you think that they'll know we're back?"

So many thoughts raced through my head—how did he know I was gone? Did he go, too? I shouldn't assume anything yet. So I asked him, "Back from where?"

"From Illinois of course. Where else?" he answered.

"Well, he doesn't know," I thought, "and I'm not ready to talk about whatever that was until I've had a chance to figure out what that was." As I rolled over, I noticed that there was absolutely no pain in my body—it was all gone.

The next few hours felt as if I was having to get reacquainted with being back in my body as if I were gone somewhere for a very long time. But where? I had already heard of the near death experience before and this tunnel that I went through with the light sure sounded like it. I said to myself "This is crazy. You can't have a near death experience without dying." I wanted to talk to somebody about this but it was too bizarre. They would think it was my imagination since I had already heard of the NDE phenomenon. Then I began to notice that I was feeling disappointment about being back in my body.

"OK, now this is going too far, I didn't die. I couldn't have been heading through a tunnel toward that fantastic light. Let me figure this out—it wasn't a dream because I wasn't asleep; it wasn't an out-of-body experience because that has happened with me a few times before and I never went through a tunnel toward a light. This was different, very different."

The next day I was depressed about being back. I didn't want to do anything, talk to anyone or go anywhere. I just wanted to be back in the bliss and the light. So I finally decided to talk to my friend, Mary, who introduced me to a video a couple of months before that about the NDE.

"I know this is going to sound bizarre but I think I had an NDE, only I didn't die," I said.

"Claire, that's not impossible, and I know someone who can help you," said Mary.

She gave me Bill Bingham's phone number, so I called right away. He invited me to an NDE support group meeting he was having at his house. He showed a video going into detail about the phenomenon where a researcher explained that there are some cases where people don't even have to die to have an NDE. It can sometimes happen when a person has received a spontaneous healing. I felt relieved to know that there have been others who have had this more unusual experience of the NDE. There is a part of me that feels a longing for that place in the light, although I cannot say exactly what is there. There is a sense of freedom, of great love, like returning home—a home that your mind may not be able to completely grasp on an earthly level, but one we all know in our hearts. I get a sense from this whole experience that I was sent into this great light to reach deeper levels of understanding of the love that God has for us, continually. I was taught or shown some thing that will open up at the right time to be put to use to help people, something that will help people during what I already know to be the time of great change for humanity.

Approximately three months after this Thanksgiving holiday and the near-death experience, the Mississippi River flooded, cresting the river countless times where no flood like that was recorded in history. The little town of Grafton, mentioned earlier that would be under water, did indeed become one of the many towns under water. Thousands of homes and businesses were destroyed, lives were lost and many left homeless. The flood was deemed "the Flood of the Millennium" by the scientists.

Something in the light lets us know that there is peace beyond the earthly circumstances. There is a choice we make to live in that peace, no matter what size the problems, trials or tribulations may be. Lasting long past the time that we spend here on earth is an eternity of love, peace and joy that few have completely known on earth, yet is available to us all. We have to be centered in it, for it is there, within us all, that peace of heaven, that light at the end of the tunnel, that heaven on earth that is not in a dollar, or a building or any material possessions, but centered in our hearts and very beings. It is the light that we are and that God created us to be.

*Claire Applegate*

# $\mathcal{A}$ Presence In My Room

*"I am an elderly woman, educated in the British Isles and Switzerland. I have a degree in Interior Design and have been running my own Interior Design business for many years. I am very down-to-earth, and not inclined to look for spiritual or deeply occult influences in my everyday life. This is why I was so taken by surprise by the following experience."*

About three years ago, after a fairly mundane ordinary day, I decided to go to bed early at about 9:30 p.m. I took a cup of tea to bed with me, and when I finished it I settled down to sleep.

After about five minutes, I had a most extraordinary experience. As I lay there in bed, listening to the noises outside, a bird chirping outside my window, a light breeze wisping through the trees and the sound of a car in the distance, I gradually became aware of a presence in my room with me.

I knew it was not a person, and I sensed it drawing near to me and hovering over me. I can only describe it as an entity, something spiritual. It enveloped me like a misty cloud, and as this happened I became aware of a sense of love, but a love I had never known in any relationship I have ever had on this earth. It encompassed me totally, settling over me gently. For a while I basked in this most marvelous sensation. Then I started to communicate with this entity. I asked it why there must be so much suffering in the world, particularly the suffering of children. The reply I received is indelibly marked in my memory:

"You must stop worrying about this—it has to happen."

Then I had full knowledge of everything. Everything was as clear as a bell. I asked no questions because I knew all the answers. With this deep love I felt absolute peace—"the peace that surpasses all understanding."

There are no words to properly describe my experience. As I read this, I am conscious that my description is totally inadequate. The encounter lasted for about 15 minutes, and then I felt the entity starting to move away. I roused myself from my taste of heaven and urged it to stay—to please not go—and if it must go to take me with it, as I could not bear to part from it. Amazingly, I sensed it was smiling in amusement, and it replied, "I must leave, but I will be back soon and I will take you with me then."

In typically human reaction I asked "How long?" "When?" "Please don't go." Slowly it left, drifting away as gently as it had come.

I told my dearest friend about this and she was fascinated. Last Saturday, March 4, 1995, she died of cancer, and she told me she was looking forward to death if that was the kind of reception that was waiting for her.

I am looking forward to death which I think opens the door to an exciting existence that awaits us as a reward for enduring the battles of this life. I tell as many people as I can about my experience as I know that it will help them to prepare for what I believe is not death but a transition to a place of love, peace and knowledge, and the successful attainment of a high spiritual level which is the perfection of the human mind.

My experience has debunked all the Christian teachings of a vengeful and angry God waiting for us with the Sword of Damocles in his hand that I had been taught by religious teachers throughout my childhood. I am certain that we will enter an existence filled with the amazing love I felt that evening at 9:30 p.m.

After the experience, I found that I had the ability to concentrate on important things like helping people in need; the more I did this, the more proficient I became as a helper. I had also lost the standards I had been taught when I was growing up to categorize people. That they were wealthy, socially important or well-bred no longer interested me. I now have friends from every walk of life, and I have become a much better person and a much more sensitive one than I was. I am also reaping a harvest of knowledge from these people, as I learn about their lives and the deep kindness that is at the heart of every human being, just waiting for someone to discover it.

I realize that I was shallow and disinterested in other people to a great extent, and I have decided that maybe that is why I was so very privileged to encounter my beautiful entity, and I shall be eternally grateful.

I am English, and Americans are right when they say we are reticent. I am not reticent any more. Now, if I love someone I tell them so. It is surprising how people react to this. It is as though they want to hear this more than anything else. I have also learned that love generates love, and it is love that is the guiding force in the afterlife. In the face of all science and advanced thinking, the sheer simplicity of the concept of love is staggering. It is all-powerful and it is so easy to do. I believe it is the initial and essential beginning to any process of higher thought and spirituality.

When I had my experience, I was not near to death. I had many sad and troubling problems involving rejection, deceit from my nearest and dearest, and monetary problems resulting from thefts. I had reached a frame of mind when I could not go on handling my own feelings. My mind had become numb and ceased to worry.

I believe that this was the reason I was receptive to the visitation that came to me. My mind had become blank from mental exhaustion, thereby opening me up to an awareness of higher thought. The conditions of my life had forced upon me a form of meditation and I was ready without realizing what was happening to me.

I came away from my experience with two concepts uppermost in my mind: love and peace. We are conditioned by this world to be suspicious and skeptical; I was no exception. Yet when I think about my communication with the spiritual entity, only one thought is consistent and dominant: it happened. I experienced it and I will never be the same again.

I did not change overnight. It took time and it is still changing me. Every day I like myself a little more. I like the change in my thinking. I like the new tolerance. I like my new ability to love my fellow man and to look for excuses for him when he steps out of line. I no longer rush to condemn. I look forward to the new religion the Bible has forecast, but I think it shall be a world-wide change in our thinking. Mankind will have ascended to a higher spiritual plane. War and violence will become anathema to us. Poverty will no longer be tolerated by us. The sick and the weak will be taken care of and loved. There will no longer be rushing around, no more traffic jams. The dollar will cease to be God. Peace and love will be new ambitions.

*Oona Cullen*

# Heavenly Visit

*"I live in Houston. I owned a poodle shop, dog grooming and supplies, for many years. I still work with dogs and enjoy their love."*

My mother gave me the most precious gift she could have given me—a chance to see her in the next life. The bonds of love were so strong that they transcended time and death.

I saw her once when I was working in the yard. I looked up and saw her sitting in the chair she always sat in. She had a transparent appearance. The date was December, 1992. She looked the same as she did before her death. She sat the same as she always sat, she even had a cigarette in her hand. I heard her say, "Penny, I'm so sorry to leave you here to do all the work by yourself." With that, she disappeared.

When she died August 30th, 1992, the bond between mother and daughter must have been strong. In life we were so close that going on alone seemed unthinkable. That heavenly visit was so beautiful. I still live with that feeling.

With her death, I was left alone except for a little dog that my mother loved. My grief was so strong that in time I may have faced my own death. But it was not my time and my mother sent for me to visit her.

On December 21, 1993, I went to bed as usual. Sleep eased my pain. In my wildest dreams, I would not have expected what was about to happen. I was waiting for her to come see me on Earth.

I felt myself traveling in darkness at a great rate of speed. I heard several messages while in darkness. One was for my aunt to check her liver. The second one was of me in a white van with a white horse. Whether it was a real horse or a saw horse, I don't remember. Next someone pinched my toe. All this I didn't see but felt, for my head was on the floorboard and my legs were over the seat. Someone said, "This one's alive but the other one's gone." After that, I will not ride in a white van, ever.

Next I saw a pinpoint of light. I could feel the speed for next the light was full vision in front of me. Such a light—brighter than any thing else I've ever seen! I can't explain how beautiful, powerful and alive it felt. It felt like pulsating rays of colors that were so vivid, some colors I've never seen before. It had a pearl-like glow about it all, radiating from the center outward.

The light filled me with a tranquil peace and a great feeling of love, a utopia that nothing could harm me in any way. I've never felt the feeling of complete love or well-being before or since. I could feel every cell in my body filling with the light of love.

My mother's face broke through the light, much like you would see a sunflower. I was not allowed to see past the light, only her hair and face. She had the most beautiful face of love and peace. She was in her early twenties, perhaps.

I could hear her voice but her lips were in a smile, not moving. She had a twinkle in her eyes.

Mother: "You are here for a visit only and will have to go back."

Me: "I don't want to go back. You look so different. Your hair and eyes are the same." I asked, "Where's Baba?" (her mother who died the year before).

Mother: "She's gone on ahead and they are preparing me to go and you will have to go back."

Me: "I don't want to go back. It's too lonely and scary there."

Mother: "You'll have to go back."

With her smile I was told that she is where she is supposed to be and I am where I'm supposed to be and everything will be okay.

When I awoke, I had a strong confused feeling and my body felt very heavy. It was an effort to walk. I remember everything. I could not believe what had happened to me. Was it a vivid dream? Dreams don't leave you changed or thinking differently. I had total recall of my experience, feelings, words, and peaceful inner love that I still carry. People noticed a change in me.

It's strange how people around you can't understand the new you. They try to get you to be your old self because your new self seems to make them uncomfortable. With time, they will accept who you are now.

I have learned what is important to me and that I matter as a valuable person. I learned so much in that brief time in the light that when we leave this earth, all we take with us is love.

I wish for that blissful feeling the experience gave me. There are days when it is hard to function. I have the feeling that I need to do more with my life but there is always something changing my plans. I've been more patient with myself, not being the perfectionist at whatever I am doing. I've learned to take life as it comes, one day at a time.

In a way I still resent having to come back. For the first time I was home where love was everything. I have no fear of dying for I know that there is another place for me and my loved ones will be there to welcome me home.

I was sent back to fulfill my destiny. I do not know the reason for my return and might never know. That is why we need to live life to its maximum each day, and being more at peace with myself.

I still miss my mother each day and I talk to her as if she were here. I know her love for me is still in my heart and mind. I want to say thanks to her for her love and her giving me a visit with her in Heaven.

Her name was Helen Drake in life. She was a person who put everyone ahead of herself, always there for anyone in need, a very special woman who loved her family and friends, who gave of herself.

God gave us a special blessing: to know that each of us is going to be fine in our new lives.

*Penny Drake*

# Alive, Well, Out of Body

*Kathryn (often called Kitty) and husband Ray, both retired, live about two miles outside of Jasper, Texas where they are members of the Trinity Episcopal Church. Because they spend part of their time in Galveston, they frequently visit St. Luke the Physician Episcopal Church. They also enjoy family, friends, bicycling, swimming and walking their Yorkie, Tibby Doll.*

It was the Spring of 1972. I was 47 years old and a teacher at an elementary school in Texas City, Texas. My husband was employed by Union Carbide Corporation in Texas City. We had three sons, two of whom were married, and one son thirteen years old. Our grandchildren lived in nearby towns with their parents. My parents were retired business people and lived in Kemah, Texas. We were happy and had no serious problems. Our adult children and their families visited us often, and our thirteen-year-old son was cooperative, friendly, and excelled in school. We attended St. George's Episcopal Church each Sunday, and at that time, I taught eight-year-old children in Sunday School.

If anyone had asked me if I were a Christian, I would have responded, "Of course. I am an Episcopalian." However, a committed Christian would have known I was a secular Christian— not a 'born again' Christian who knew the Lord and hoped to spend eternity with him. A committed 'born again' would have known I was headed straight for Hell, though I considered myself to be a good person. And they would have been correct.

My husband had committed his life to the Lord in a Baptist Church as a teenager. He believed in Jesus but had not matured into a strong enough believer to share his faith with me, with our children, or with other people.

I had doubt that God really existed. I attended church because I thought churches were good institutions, and the world

145

was better off with them than without them. Therefore, I decided we should support them with our presence and financially but not with too much time and money. I knew there were richer folks than we who liked to give their money, and five dollars a week of our money was enough for the church.

As a child, each Sunday I was sent to Trinity Episcopal Church in Galveston where we lived. I knew a few Bible stories, but I wasn't sure anyone really believed them. I had never read a Bible. There may not have been one in my home. One of my minors in college was English, and I had read the works of many great authors but had not been introduced to The Holy Bible; so it was unimportant to me.

My life drifted along in an ordinary, uncomplicated, socially acceptable way that gave one hour a week to church and $5 to God. I was a happy, politically correct person, I thought.

One Sunday after church I was chatting with a lady who taught the Sunday School Class for eleven-year-old children. She told me about an Episcopal church in Houston named The Church of Redeemer. She said she had attended that church as a child, but since then the church had deteriorated into unchristian chaos. She said the people who attended the church now spoke and sang in tongues, healed people with prayer, and claimed the Lord talked to them and guided and directed their lives. She said she would never go to that church again.

I asked about the location of the church; for she had aroused my curiosity, and I wanted to see the services for myself. I hadn't seen anything like that in our church.

Upon inquiry I was told The Church of the Redeemer held prayer and praise services each Friday night at seven o'clock. I talked my husband into going with me because the church was located in an old part of Houston, and the safety of the area was questionable. We left home early to give us plenty of time to locate the church, and we had no trouble finding it. Being thirty minutes early, we decided to wait in the church. We chose seats several rows from the front on the far left side, thinking this would give us a better view of the show we were about to witness. We were the only ones in the church when a priest entered and came toward us. He introduced himself and asked us our names. We conversed with him but did not tell him we had come merely out of curiosity, so I was surprised when he told us he hoped we would find what we were looking for. How could he think we were looking for something?

The church was large. The front walls were covered by an enormous mural depicting people from all walks of life looking with adoration at a huge Jesus. In front of the mural was an altar and chairs for a choir. Not only could this large church seat people on the lower floor, there was also a fairly good-sized balcony that could be used.

I had no idea the church would fill up, but it did. After filling the first floor and balcony, people sat on the floor around the altar. As they entered, they greeted each other with hugs and phrases like 'Praise the Lord' and 'Praise Jesus,' definitely peculiar for Episcopalians but nice, gentle, and orderly. I decided they must all be very close friends to be so familiar, but this was not true, because some of them came to us and hugged us. Those folks seemed to love everybody.

Soon everyone was seated. A group of folks with guitars, drums, cymbals, and tambourines gathered around the piano at the front. Church began with lots of happy music.

We were not disappointed. Everything possible happened during that service. With hands lifted, the people praised the Lord and sang in tongues—the loveliest *a Capella* music I have ever heard. They prophesied, gave words of knowledge, testified of healings, spoke in tongues and gave translations. All of this was done with dignity, the glory being given to God. But most of all, their expressions impressed me. With great sincerity they were adoring their Lord, just as the people in the mural were pictured. I wondered how they could love Jesus so much, since he had died 2000 years ago and they couldn't see Him. I realized I was watching a depth of love and worship I had never seen, much less experienced.

At nine o'clock the people were still praising the Lord, and we left because we had a 60 mile drive home.

The next day, Saturday, I went to visit my parents in Kemah, about fifteen miles away. As I drove down the highway, I thought about the worship service at The Church of the Redeemer.

I recalled the facial expressions on the faces and in the eyes of the people so obviously in love with Jesus, whom they worshipped as though He were alive, able to hear them, and present among them. Suddenly I said aloud, "Jesus, if you really do exist, please show me." HE DID!

In an instant I found myself in another place, and I was with Jesus. We did not talk with words from our mouths, but we communicated rapidly with thoughts. I was aware of being surrounded and filled with a love I have no words to describe. A very long distance below, I saw my car on Highway 146. I could look through the roof of it at my body. The car was traveling down the road. Jesus must have been steering it, because I did not think my body could drive the car without me. I saw other traffic, but I told Him I had better get back to my body because I did not want to have a wreck and hurt someone. I realize now that was a dumb thing to tell Him, but I am a practical person and thought I should be in the car doing my job even though I was thoroughly enjoying my visit with the Lord. In an instant, I was in my body and everything was as usual except for one thing. I knew Jesus was alive, and I had given my life to Him. I was 'born again,' a new person ready to make a new beginning. I was filled with a joy I had never experienced, and I was in love with Jesus.

I went on to Kemah to visit my parents but did not tell them my experience. This is something I have told very few people. I told my husband and the Rector of our church. Both of them were supportive.

It is important to me that people who read or hear about my out-of-body experience understand that it was not a near-death experience, because I was alive and in very good health when it happened. Also, it was not an experience I was seeking in order to relax or meditate. I had no idea this sort of thing could happen to me. Very simply, I had asked a question, and Jesus had chosen to answer it in this way.

I have discovered that a lot of people have experiences with Jesus, but they are not all alike. I don't know why. It's none of my business; it's His. He is in the business of saving souls. I am only an elementary school teacher, now retired. So far this is the only out-of-body experience I have had.

Naturally, this experience had a tremendous effect on my life. I was filled with love and joy. This love and joy overflowed into my work, my family, and everyone I met. I set my clock for 5:00 a.m. so I would have time to read the Bible and talk to Jesus. I read a great variety of religious books. I began to give a tithe (10%) of my income to the church. I willingly gave my time to the church. I now knew without a doubt that our spirits are separate from our bodies and will live forever though our bodies will die. I knew that with Jesus in eternity I would experience His wonderful love and joy forever.

After about four months, my newly found love and joy began to fade. No matter how much I cried out to Jesus, the fire was slowly dying. I was devastated.

It was at that point that I read *Nine O'clock In The Morning* by Dennis Bennett and *They Speak With Other Tongues* by John Sherrill. They both told about the Baptism of the Holy Spirit and the gifts and the fruits that resulted. I read and reread the Book of Acts and 1st and 2nd Corinthians trying to learn all I could about the Holy Spirit. Apparently He was alive and still giving His fruits and gifts to God's people, if they wanted them.

I decided I did want the Holy Spirit and His gifts and fruits in my life, but I wasn't sure how to get them. I began by confessing my sins on my knees at 5 o'clock every morning. This took about three months because I confessed every little sin I could think of—even little things like not answering my mom even though I heard her calling one time when I was four years old. I had accumulated forty-seven years of unconfessed large and small sins, and I wanted my spirit to be as clean as possible. Then one day, I knew it was time to talk to Jesus about His Holy Spirit.

I came in from school one afternoon. No one was home. I sat in a chair on the patio, and I told Jesus I was ready for Him to Baptize me with His Holy Spirit if He wanted to.

That was all it took. I was zapped! The joy and love returned. A feeling I call electricity filled my body from head to toe. I was aware of the presence of invisible spirits all around me, dancing and rejoicing. I joined them. For at least two hours I danced and sang in other tongues. I cannot begin to describe the wonder of these moments.

After a year the constant feeling of being electrified diminished, but never completely or forever. I have learned that it is one of the ways in which the Holy Spirit communicates with me. Sometimes it means I should pray a certain way or for a certain person, or it sometimes verifies that something is true. He helps me with everything. If I wonder if I should buy something, a 'quickening' of the Spirit means 'yes.' He has helped me know when to speak at meetings, what clothes to buy, what house to buy, and so forth. He is interested in everything that happens to me and everything I do. He has made His presence known during stressful times—a car wreck, cancer surgery. He has healed me, comforted me, given me courage, and He never lets me forget Jesus.

Many books have been written about the gifts and fruits of the Holy Spirit, and I experienced some of them. These gifts and fruits are not only helpful to the individual blessed with them, but the Holy-Spirit-filled person is equipped to use these gifts in his church and everywhere he goes. It is not a selfish thing. In fact, I believe a selfish person would lose this blessing.

I am not better than anyone else, but I am a better person than I was and fully realize the great value of each spirit on this earth, and that includes everyone—rich, poor, retarded, average, brilliant, black, white, yellow, good, bad, insane, criminal—EVERYONE! It is only through the power of the Holy Spirit and the grace of God that I can love and care about everyone.

I have a folder of supernatural happenings that have taken place in my life since the out-of-body experience. They would fill many pages. The out-of-body experience was a beginning of many things to come, not an end in itself.

*Kathryn Haire*

# Witness to an Ascension

*Ms. Reaben is president of Dupli-Tapes Film and Video and is president of Cinema Texas Media Productions, Houston, Texas. She graduated from the University of St. Thomas with a B.A. in Art. Ms. Reaben is also a professional artist, photographer and writer.*

In 1956, I was 14 years old when my new half brother James E. Reaben was born. We had the same mother but different fathers. Being an only child all my life, I was thrilled to have him here. Little did I know that he would later give me a great gift— a glimpse into the process of crossing over to the other side.

At the moment Jimmy entered this world, my life had been filled with excitement and adventure. I, naively, thought Jimmy's life would be the same. While my life has certainly had its moments of pain, the joys have always been much greater. With Jimmy, it was the exact opposite—the agony of life seemed to outweigh the joy. Success has always come easily for me, but for him, it was illusive until the last three years of his life. Our lives would always remain in sharp contrast.

Jimmy, as a small child, liked to hunt the ditches for frogs and crawdads, finding delight in creatures that swam in the water and climbed in the trees. He also liked to paint. I knew he was destined for an artist's life when, at the age of 6, he placed a canvas on the ground, climbed up in a tree and threw paint down on it. As he got older, his artistic talents would grow to describe the actions, feelings and foresight into his life and death at the age of 33.

While there were vast differences between us, there was a spiritual and psychic bond that was timeless. For instance, I would think an action-type thought and Jimmy would respond. I remember one summer day, Jimmy and I were lounging by the side of a swimming pool when I thought to myself, "I wish someone would go in the house and get my shoes so I can go home." Jimmy, who was about 9 years old at the time, promptly got up, said not a word and left. A few minutes later he returned carrying my shoes and said, "You wanted these?"

Sometimes, our psychic bond took the form of dreams. Once, I dreamed that Jimmy was riding his bicycle in the Montrose Area of Houston with his friend Marsha, when a car—not seeing them—hit Jimmy. I was not surprised when a few months later, my mother called me from a hospital to tell me Jimmy had been hit by a car while riding his bicycle on the very street where I saw the accident, and with the friend I saw in the dream. He would be alright. The dream was another reinforcement for the validity of the hundreds of psychic communications between us.

As Jimmy grew up, he experienced emotional trauma, pain and self-doubt from teachers who punished him because he was dyslexic and hyperactive. As a result, his self-esteem plummeted. Consequently, he was in and out of many schools because of an inability to adjust. The type of schools he attended were as chaotic as his life—public schools, a school for the retarded (no place else would take him at the time even though his intelligence was above average), a ranch-type school with a military regimen, a school for artistic types and then, finally, back to public schools. His father, an engineer, added to his fragile psychological state by continually telling him he was a failure—from the time Jimmy was a small boy. His self-esteem and psychological state plummeted from derision by his father, but it was offset by our mother and me. We believed in his artistic talents and in his ability to achieve. Slowly, his art began to flower. When he was a young teenager, I took his paintings to juried art shows and never told them he wasn't an adult. Not only were they accepted, they were sold.

By the time he was 30, major Houston galleries were taking a serious look at this young artist who expressed his rebellion against the way society and authority figures had treated him. Numerous newspaper and magazine articles began to appear praising this young artist's unusual way of painting his internal fears—often with a sardonic sense of humor. Representation by Moody Gallery in Houston secured his reputation and widened his appeal; his work began to make its way into major museum and private collections.

Around that same time, I began having forewarning dreams about his impending death. The dreams did not show me how he would die, just that the process was about to begin. I quickly discounted them and tried to reason them out of my mind. It simply was not possible that Jimmy, whose life had been a struggle since birth, could die so young. The denial within myself stopped when, in 1987, Jimmy discovered he had AIDS.

The turmoil began. With death a certainty, Jimmy began to paint with the fury and intensity of a speeding locomotive. Our family, while already in a state of chaos, went into hyper-chaos when Jimmy's father died. My mother, then 72, was dealing with the death of her husband and with her only son dying of AIDS. Her older sister was critically ill and near death, too. My personal and business life were a mess as well. It seemed there was a hurricane running through all of our lives and I was at the center of it. My mother, leaning heavily on me to solve each new crisis added more weight to my already overburdened psyche. Only God's light saved my sanity and got me through the turmoil of my soul.

Jimmy's fear of life had always been great, but his fear of death was even greater. To fight the demons within himself, he began to paint his fears of death with intensity- pouring out his feelings and emotions onto paper, canvas and wood. The colors were dark and foreboding. The subjects were sarcophaguses with bloody eyes, Egyptian gateways to the other side, and into the unknown. One of his paintings, a self-portrait, showed his mouth open, screaming in rage and terror at himself, AIDS and his inevitable death.

As AIDS began to capture his body and his brain, he became partially paralyzed. Determined to keep going and to complete as many paintings as he could before he died, he began painting with his left hand, as his right hand was now paralyzed. Awkwardly, and with incredible beauty, he executed a magnificent series of 31 gold and pen paintings entitled "Death Threats." The Museum of Fine Arts in Houston purchased this series, painted on top of pages from an old chemistry notebook from the 1930's. The last in the series was a gate to heaven, filled with gold light.

These predictive paintings represented not only the psychological acceptance of his fate but also the spiritual renewal and rebirth of his consciousness. Life on the other planes had become his friend and not his enemy.

AIDS began to advance quickly and eradicate his neurological functions. He lost his ability to walk and his ability to move his arms. The function of the right hand was already gone and now he lost the function of his left hand, only able to wiggle one finger. He began losing his ability to speak and went from slurring speech to an inability to form words to a primitive "uh". AIDS, cruelly, began to attack his vision. During the last few weeks week of his life his vision began to disappear. It also attacked his swallowing mechanism and he could no longer eat. Fluid began to build up in his lungs and he gurgled as he struggled for air.

It was Thursday, June 30, 1989. In New Orleans, an exhibit of Jimmy's art was being shown at a prestigious gallery. The show had been on for about 2 months and Friday was the last day of the show. Jimmy, nor none of the family had seen it. Since I own a video production company, I, along with a friend, decided to fly over and video tape the show. While I knew he couldn't see it when I brought it back, I knew I could describe it to him. I told him I was leaving and that I would be back the next day. It would be the last time I would see him in the physical world, but not the last time I would be with him.

After a long shooting day at the art gallery, I went back to the hotel and fell asleep quickly. The room at the Hilton was comfortable and I slept soundly until I was awakened by a vision in the early morning hours. I saw Jimmy, out of his bed, sitting on top of a lavatory in his hospital room, leaning over and wanting to throw up. He was ready and waiting for some kind of signal that he could leave this life.

He asked me for a container. Looking around the room, I saw a small, plastic trash can and asked him if it would do. It was clean, I told him, except for a few things I had already discarded in it. "Was it alright?" I asked.

He nodded his acceptance and I placed the receptacle on the floor, under his head. In his shy, sweet way, he looked longingly at me, with a sense of anticipation that his burdens were about to be released. I remember that there was a mirror behind him. It seemed his hair was filled with the blond curls he had as a child.

Across the room sat a nun in full habit, with only her radiant face showing. Her eyes were kind and filled with love for Jimmy. There was a gentle smile on her face as she sat, not moving. It was as if she had been waiting with Jimmy for a long time. I sensed her mission was to be by Jimmy's side until he was ready to leave and to help in his transition.

The nun looked at Jimmy and smiled widely. With the innocence of a two year old boy and the wisdom of the ancients, he looked back at her and said, "Is it alright for me to go now?" Her aura was as bright as a full moon and with a gentle voice that seemed to echo the universe, she said, "Yes, my child, you may leave now." Assured, Jimmy leaned over the trash can and an electric white liquid poured from his mouth.

Tears began to form in my eyes because I knew the finality of what I had just witnessed. I glanced at the clock and saw that it was about 5:00 am. I woke my friend to tell him Jimmy had just died and to expect a call from Mother shortly. Quickly, I brushed the tears from my eyes and stifled my cries so as not to break my last moments with Jimmy in grief. I knew that he was allowing me to be with him as he transcended and I wanted to witness his moment of greatest ecstasy.

Before my eyes were barely shut, the vision was back. There was Jimmy, standing in the middle of a busy downtown street, much like the city where he lived, Houston. While he seemed humbled and filled with melancholy as he took this last opportunity to look at the daily life of man on earth, he was also filled with inner strength and acceptance. His eyes were like an eagle's as he perceived and absorbed every color, shape and movement of humanity, committing it to soul memory.

He began to walk across the street but there were no people on Jimmy's side of the street—only on the other side, opposite him. As he approached the white stripe in the center, he turned into a one dimensional image, much like a stiff paper doll. He bent over from the waist and a white, cloud-like mass shot up from the base of his spine and he vanished from mankind.

Regressing back to the Creator, he quickly appeared in a different form. In the movie screen of my mind appeared a large incubator, roomy and spacious. It was pink, inside and out and so was Jimmy, now a newborn baby. He was lying on his back, gazing up at a star-filled sky, his eyes filled with wonderment. There was deep, ancient knowing in his soul as he waited for the next portal to open in his cosmic flight to God's galaxy.

A beam of light came down from the heavens and lifted the newborn up and carried him into the distant darkness of the heavens, beyond the boundaries of time. There appeared, far away in my vision, a quivering energy form of undulating rainbows, waiting patiently for its child to return. I could see the light beam, carrying Jimmy, moving fast across the beyond, towards this monolithic energy form. Jimmy immediately began to transform into a light form himself, vibrating with electricity and color, so very much alive. As he flew towards the other energy form, Jimmy recognized its warmth and comfort from long ago. The two met and wrapped their soul arms around one another; ecstatically, they melted into one giant ball of light. Exploding with love, the fireworks of the heavens began.

The energy produced by them was so far-reaching, it traveled all the way to my heart and I burst with joy. But only for a moment, for the love reached my eyes and washed my face with tears. Sobbing by now, I sat up as I heard the phone ring. It was mother calling from Houston. In a clear and calm voice she said "Jimmy is gone." I replied, "Yes, I know."

*Gail Reaben Moseley*

*POST SCRIPT: Currently, a documentary film titled "Whole Sky Burning" is being made on the life of James E. Reaben.*

# ife After Birth

*Ray Mullen serves as a sex offender therapist in Houston, Texas.*

It was 5:00 a.m., June 1, 1976 and a cool darkness had closed in around the old 24 Hour club of Alcoholics Anonymous in Austin, Texas. Everyone had gone home but me. I nibbled on a cheese sandwich prescribed by a member and awaited the morning arrival of men who were to take me to the Austin State Hospital.

A few hours before I had literally crawled to the club in a weakened condition. Some honey mixed with orange juice was given me by a nurse named Arlene. She had also made the cheese sandwich and diagnosed my problem as hypoglycemia.

A number of people sat up with me for hours sharing their experience, strength, and hope. I wondered about their motives. How could they possibly understand my situation? What did they want? They said they were there because of me. How could that be? I noted a wooden plaque on the wall which read, "ABANDON ALL HOPE, YE WHO ENTER HERE..."— Dante. That made sense. I was thirty-six years old, penniless, unemployed, homeless, friendless. Recovery seemed remote and improbable. I had considered suicide but something blocked that path. With each nibble of the sandwich I gagged with nausea, my head was pounding. I was tired but every time I tried to sleep a loud shotgun-like auditory hallucination awakened me.

I walked out into the morning. A light mist floated over the yard softening the silhouettes of the trees below a moonless sky filled with a billion stars. I searched for and found the ever-risen star of the north and watched as Venus, the morning star, peeked over the horizon to herald the dawn. And then the dawn, as I remembered from Hamlet, in scarlet mantle clad, crept o'er yon high eastward hill. The hill was but the house next door as there were no hills to the east.

As I stood there I was suddenly overwhelmed by a feeling of peace and hope. Somehow I knew at that moment my life had changed gloriously and there would be no going back. In all the years that have followed that feeling has never really left me. As I went back into the building I noted the plaque now said, "God grant me the serenity to accept the things I can not change, the courage to change the things I can, and the wisdom to know the difference."

I can not explain how my whole life changed in a moment that day. I assume a power greater than myself caused that to be. Perhaps the good life was always there and I was given the power that day to see what had so long eluded me.

*Ray Mullen*

# Experiencer Questionnaire

1. Do You Believe in a Heaven as described in the Bible?

   Yes ___ No ___

2. Do you believe in a judgement by God?

   Yes ___ No ___

3. Do you believe in reincarnation?

   Yes ___ No ___

4. Did your beliefs change after your NDE-Mystical Experience?

   Yes ___ No ___

5. Are you convinced that your beliefs are right?

   Yes ___ No ___

6. How do you explain the differences in beliefs?

   _____

   _____

   _____

   _____

   _____

7. What questions would you like added to this questionnaire?

   _____

   _____

   _____

_____

_____

_____

8. What do you think were the most important
   things you learned from your experience?

   _____

   _____

   _____

   _____

   _____

9. If you could get one idea across to others based
   on what your experience taught you, what would
   it be?

   _____

   _____

   _____

   _____

   _____

   _____

# Epilog

*"Part of a true person is inside time, and part is beyond time. The time part dies. The other part is the good friend of forever."*[1]

Now that we have learned that there is nothing to fear in death, we as near-death and mystical conversion experiencers must fit this brain-blowing event into our old everyday lives. Our lives have been radically and suddenly changed in mind and soul, if not body. Everyone around us is the same as before. How do we relate? How to explain? How to be?

We've had a glimpse of eternal consciousness and lost all fear of death. Some of us had a taste of unconditional love which, for the moment, at least banished *all* fear.

Love and fearlessness — these are the tools we all need to remember to use in navigating through the rest of our lives. If we don't fear the loss of life, why should we fear anything in it? Fear diminishes our ability to love. It is only fear that keeps the presence of the love we now know from expressing itself.

Some experiencers spend decades in anguish trying to puzzle out what they were sent back to accomplish in life. For many, it was mentioned during their experience, if they could only remember and make sense of it.

I submit that we have been given the tools to be more accepting, forgiving and loving. To love more and fear less *is* the accomplishment. It is the continuing work. Keep in touch with that love inside you. Know that your brother has it, too. Know that we are all connected at that inner point.

*The open secret*　　　　　　　*But ecstatic love*
*Many mystics have extolled:*　*Comes to many,*
*Fear not death*　　　　　　　*Probably all*
*Live bold for*　　　　　　　　*In that timeless,*
*Death comes not*　　　　　　　*Eternal enthrall.*
*To the old or any*

---

1　Barks, Coleman. *Delicious Laughter.* Athens, GA: Maypop Books, 1990.

# Support Groups

## IANDS (International Association of Near-Death Studies) Active Groups

### Canada

**British Columbia**
Vancouver: Christopher Lovelidge, 604-543-7446
Victoria: Christopher Kunz, 604-386-9208

**Ontario**
Ottawa: Marion Tapp, 613-728-9199

### United States of America

IANDS, the International Association of Near-Death Studies, Inc. P.O. Box 502, East
Windsor Hill, CT 06028-0502 (203) 528-4144

**Arizona**
Tucson: Carlene Huesgen, 602-325-1107

**California**
Bay Area: Diana Schmidt, 510-234-4125
Beverly Hills: Darlene Jaman, 213-935-9354
Fountain Valley: Diane Craig, 714-968-9502
La Mesa: Patti White, 619-465-0490
San Diego: Vanessa Edwards, 619-453-3945
San Francisco: Rosa Lea Newsom Linsom, 619-453-3945
San Jose: Barbara Heather, 408-264-3336
Santa Fe Springs: Dianne Morrissey, 310-692-6556

**Connecticut**
Greater Hartford: Sandra Procko, 860-677-9586

**Florida**
Ft Lauderdale: Jack Cuthrell, 1199 S. Lala Dr. #11, Lantana 33462
W. Palm Beach: Cathy Clark, 407-790-2995

**Georgia**
Warner Robins: Sue Ellen Davis, 106-D Memorial Ter 31093

**Idaho**
Heyburn: Lori Fitzhugh, 208-678-7223

**Kansas**
Kansas City area: Sue Wilson, 9309 W 81st, Overland Park 66204

**Kentucky**
Butler: Anne Hosking, 606-472-2131

**Massachusetts**
Boston area: Joanne Hager, 617-232-4500

**Missouri**
St. Louis: Peggy Raso, 314-524-7833

**New Jersey**
Belle Mead: Donna McGrath, 908-281-6888
Lindenwold: Lynne/Dan Campbell, 609-783-2741

## New York
Long Island: Rachel Cohen, 516-794-1223
New York City: Julie Levine, 718-789-8157
Rochester: Donna LaDuqe, 716-467-0704
## Ohio
Akron/Canton: John & Barbara Eastmena, 216-494-2963
Cincinnati: Marty & Valerie Chandler, 513-851-0557
Columbus: Nancy Clark, 614-873-5307
## Oklahoma
616-882-9912
## Oregon
Portland East: Tricia Richie, 503-282-6455
Portland East: Sharon Sternberg, 503-254-9236
Portland West: Debbie Gregg, 910-299-0067
## Pennsylvania/New Jersey
NE Philadelphia: Beverly Brodsky, 215-677-2507
Pittsburgh: Julia Gibson, 412-481-8180
## Texas
Austin: Shannon Heller, 512 443-9778 or 512 328-5416
Houston: Bill Bingham, 713-464-1458
Lubbock: Joanna Reed, 806-745-3761
San Antonio: Debbie James, 210-684-8419
## Utah
Salt Lake City: Lynn Johnson, 801-261-1412
## Virginia
District of Columbia: Maggie Callahan, 703-860-8464
Dictrict of Columbia: Diane Corcoran, 703-476-1944
Richmond: Margaret Denvil, 804-353-5430
## Washington
Olympia: Norma Hissong, 360-705-0161
Seattle: Kimberly Clark Sharp, 206-932-4848
Seattle: Greg Wilson, 206-525-5489
Tacoma: Maura Casson, 206-984-0635
Tacoma: Barbara Springer, 206-531-0087
## West Virginia
Wheeling: Richard Dinges, 304-547-0943

## A Course in Miracles - Major Teaching Centers
Foundations for a Course in Miracles
RR 2 Box 71
Roscoe, NY 12776-9506
(607) 498-4116

## Circle of Atonement
Box 4238
W. Sedona, AZ 86340
(520) 282-0790

# Electronic Forums

*Internet searches with different but similar words will result in different lists. Try NDE, NDE's, Near-Death Experience, Near-Death Experiences, and so forth for best results.*

**Fearless**
http://198.68.36.114/GIB/befaft/B&A-4.html

**IANDS England**
10014.1637@compuserve.com

**IANDS Website**
http://www.iands.org

**Index**
http://www.well.com/user/bobby/

**Life After Life**
http://www.nando.net/ads/gift/videos/v3560.html

**The Miracle Network**
http://www.lightworks.com/Connections/MiracleNetwork

**An Online Natural Death Handbook:**
http://www.newciv.org/GIB/natdeath/ndh3.html#SECTION45

**Out Of Body Experiences**
http://www.linknet.it/Spirit/obe.html

**The WWW Virtual Library: Archive X, Paranormal Phenomena**
http://www.crown.net/X/NDE.html


See also forums on CompuServe, America OnLine and others.

# Bibliography

*A Course In Miracles*. Tiburon, Ca. Foundation for Inner Peace, 1975. A self-study course in spiritual psychotherapy.

Alvarado, C. "Trends in the Study of Out-of-Body Experiences"*: Journal of Scientific Exploration*, 1989; 3:1:27-42. An overview of trends, developments since 19th century.

Atwater, P.M.H. *Beyond the Light: What Isn't Being Said About The Near-Death Experience*. NY: Birch Lane, 1994; NY: Avon Books, 1995 and *Coming Back to Life*. NY: Dodd, Mead & Co., 1988. Personal observation and inquiry about after-effects and experiencer reactions.

Barks, Coleman. *Delicious Laughter*. Athens, GA: Maypop Books, 1990. Poetry of Rumi.

Bascor, Lionel C. and B. Loccher. *By The Light*. NY: Avon, 1995. About true stories of NDE and how they changed the lives of the experiencers.

Basford, Terry. *Near-Death Experiences: An Annotated Bibliography*. NY: Garland, 1990. Very thorough bibliography.

Berger, Arthur (ed.) *Perspectives on Death and Dying: Cross-Cultural and Multi-Disciplinary Views*. Philadelphia, PA: Charles Press, 1989. Death and cross-cultural studies, attitudes toward death.

Blackmore, Susan. *Beyond the Body*. London, England: Heinneman, 1982. Investigations about NDE survivors and *Dying To Live: Science and the Near-Death Experience*. London: Grafton/HarperCollins, 1993. Non-mystical explanations of NDE as a product of brain function.

Bluebond-Langner, M. *The Private Worlds of Dying Children*. Princeton University Press, 1978. NDE's in children.

Brinkley, Damion. *Saved By The Light*. NY: Random House. 1994. Biographical NDE; and *At Peace In The Light*. NY: Villard Books, 1995. True story of a man who died and the revelations he received.

Brown, Mary T. Life After Death. NY: Ballantine, 1994. "Psychic" reveals what happens to us when we die.

Callanan, Maggie and Patricia Kelley. *Final Gifts*. NY: Simon & Schuster, 1992. Hospice nurses describe experiences of the dying for caregivers and family.

Cox-Chapman, Mally. *The Case for Heaven*. NY: Putnam, 1995. Cultural presuppositions about Heaven and relationship to NDE's.

Cressy, Judith. *Near-Death Experience: Mysticism or Madness*. Hanover, MA: Christopher, 1994. Includes suggestions for caregivers.

Crookall, R. *Out-of-Body Experiences: A Fourth Analysis*. NY: Carol Publishing Group, 1991. Library of the mystic arts.

Currie, Ian. *You Cannot Die: The Incredible Findings of a Century of Research on Death*. NY: Methuen, 1978. Conclusions and opinions.

Doore, G. *What Survives? Contemporary Explorations of Life After Death*. Los Angeles, CA: Jeremy P. Tarcher, 1990. Future life, death, materialism.

Dossey, Larry, MD. *Space, Time and Medicine*. Boulder, CO: Shambhala, 1979. See also *Recovering the Soul: A Scientific and Spiritual Search*. NY: Bantam, 1989. Spirituality in medicine and healing.

Eadie, Betty. *Embraced by the Light*. Placerville, CA: Gold Leaf Press, 1992. Biographical experience.

Easwaran, Eknath. *The Upanishads*. Tomales, CA: Niligri Press, 1987.Early Hindu spiritualists.

Farr, Sydney. *What Tom Sawyer Learned From Dying*. Norfolk, VA: Hampton Roads, 1993. Biographical.

Flynn, Charles P. *After The Beyond: Human Transformation and the Near-Death Experience*. Englewood Cliffs, NJ: Prentice-Hall, 1985.

Foundation For Inner Peace. *A Course in Miracles*. Tiburea, CA: Viking, 1995. A self-study course in spiritual psychotherapy.

Frederick Franck, M.D. *The Book of Angelus Silesius*. NY: Random House, 1978. Poetry of Angelus Silesius.

Gabbard, G. O. "Do Near-Death Experiences Occur Only Near Death?" *Journal of Nervous and Mental Diseases,* 169:374-77. 1981. Exploration of a basic question in the field.

Gabbard, G., and S. Tremlow. *Within the Eyes of the Mind: An Empiric Analysis of Out-of-Body States*. Praeger, 1984.

Gallup, George Jr. *Adventures in Immortality*. NY: McGraw-Hill, 1982. Study of American beliefs about life after death, with statistics.

Godwin, Joscelyn. *Harmonies of Heaven and Earth*. Rochester, VT: Inner Traditions Int. Ltd., 1987. Music and spirituality.

Grey, Margot. *Return from Death: An Exploration of the Near-Death Experience*. London & New York: Arkana, 1985. Inquiries after the fact.

Grey, Margot and Bush, Nancy. Distressing Near-Death Experiences. *Psychiatry,* 55 February, 1992. About accounts of negative experiences.

Greyson, Bruce. Clinical Approaches to the Near-Death Experience. *Journal of Near-Death Studies,* 1987; 6 (1); 4152. What can we say?

Greyson, Bruce and Charles P. Flyn, Eds. *The Near-Death Experience: Problems, Prospects, Perspectives.* Springfield, IL: Charles C. Thomas, 1984. For source material and research.

Grof, Stansilav and Christina. *Beyond Death: The Gates of Consiousness.* NY: Thames & Hudson, 1980. Cross-cultural.

Grosso, Michael. *The Final Choice.* Walpole, NH: Stillpoint Publishing, 1985.

Hampe, Johann. *To Die Is To Gain: The Experience of One's Own Death.* Atlanta, GA: John Knox, 1978. European information.

Harpur, Tom. *Life After Death.* Toronto: McClelland & Stewart, 1992. General information with religious overtones from ethics columnist.

Harris, Barbara and Lionel C. Bascom. *The Near-Death Experience and Beyond.* NY: Pocket Books. 1990. About accounts of the NDE.

*The Holy Bible.* Acts 9:1-30, Corinthians 12:1-7, Ezekiel 1, Isaiah 6, Mark 1:9-13. Various translations.

Irwin, H. J. *Flight of Mind.* Psychological Study of the Out-of-Body Experience. Metucheu, NJ: Scarecrow Press, 1985. Astral projection.

James, William. *Varieties of Religious Experience.* NY: Triumph Books, 1991. Classic study of wide range of spiritual experiences.

Josephs, A. "Hemingway's Out-of-Body Experience." *Hemingway Review,* 1983; 2(2): 11-17. About an experience of Heminway's and the effects on his writings.

Jovanovich, Pierre. *An Inquiry Into The Existence of Guardian Angels.* Translated by Stephen Becker. Evans, 1995.

Jung, Carl. *Memories, Dreams, Reflections.* NY: Vintage, 1965. Contains his autobiographical account of an NDE.

Kasma-Glin-Pa (transl. by Robert A. F. Thurman). *Tibetan Book of the Dead.* NY: Bantam Books, 1993. Tibetan spiritual practices especially related to physical death.

Kastenbauem, Robert (ed). Between Life and Death. Vol. 1, *Springer Series on Death and Suicide.* NY: Springer, 1979. Eight professionals examine NDE's and other phenomena.

Kirscher, Pamela, M.D. *Love is the Link.* Birdett, NY: Larson Publications, 1995. Experiences as a hospice doctor.

Knox, Jean. *Death and Dying.* NY: Chelsea House Publishers, 1989. Dying with dignity, grief.

Krishnan, V. Near-Death Experiences: Evidence for Survival. *Anabiosis: The Journal For Near-Death Studies* (Spring), 1985; 5:1:21-38.

Kubler-Ross, Elizabeth. *On Death and Dying*. NY: MacMillan Publishers, 1969. See also *On Life After Death*. Berkeley CA: Celestial Arts, 1991. Classic on death-bed experiences.

Kubler-Ross, Elizabeth and Lorimer, David. *Whole in One: The Near-Death Experience and the Ethic of Interconnectedness*. London: Viking Penguin, 1990. Philosophical inquiries.

Lewis, James R. *Encyclopedia of Afterlife Beliefs and Phenomena*. Foreword by Raymond Moody. Detroit, MI: Gale Research, 1994. A collection of beliefs and traditions around the world.

Lundahl, Craig. *A Collection of Near-Death Research Readings: Scientific Inquiries into the Experiences of Persons Near Physical Death*. Chicago, IL: Nelson Hall, 1982. Includes long history of NDE's among Mormons.

Maurice, M.D. *Beyond Death's Door*. NY: Bantam Books, 1979. Fundamental slant on NDE's.

Mitchell, J. *Out-of-Body Experiences: A Handbook*. Jefferson, NC: McFarland, 1981. See also "Out-of-Body Experiences and Physician." *The Osteopathic Physician*, 1983; 41:44-49. For the medical set.

Monroe, R. A. *Journeys Out of the Body*. NY: Doubleday, 1977. Astral projection. Music can be related.

Moody, Raymond A., Jr. M.D. *Life After Life? The Investigation of a Phenomenon: Survival of Bodily Death*. Atlanta, GA: Stackpole Books, 1976. The beginning of the popularization of mystical experience. The term 'NDE' first used in this book.

Moody, Raymond A., Jr. M.D. *Reflections on Life After Life*. Atlanta, GA: Mockingbird Books, 1977. Questions on the first book.

Moody, Raymond A., Jr. M.D. and P. Perry. *The Light Beyond*. NY: Bantam, 1988. The book that started the inquiries.

Moolenburgh, H.C., M.D. *Handbook of Angels*. Essex, England: C.W. Daniel Company, Limited, 1984. Hard to find.

Morse, Melvin, M.D. *Closer to the Light: Learning From the Near-Death Experiences of Children*. NY: Villard, 1990. NDE's in children. See also *Transformed by the Light: The Powerful Effect of Near-Death Experiences on People's Lives*. NY: Villard Books, 1992.

Morse, M., Castilo, P., Venecia, D., Milstein, J., and D. C. Tyler. Childhood Near-Death Experiences. *American Journal of Diseases of Children* (November), 1986; 140:1110-14. All about the childhood NDE.

Morse, M., Conner, D., and D. Tyler. Near-Death Experiences in a Pediatric Population. American *Journal of Diseases of Children* (June) 1989; 139:595-600. Children's NDE's.

Morse, M., Venecia, D., and J. Milstein. Near-Death Experiences: A Neurophysiologic Explanatory Model. *Journal of Near-Death Studies,* 1989; 8:45-53. Brain chemistry explanation.

Myers, F. W. H. "Human Personality and Its Survival of Bodily Death." Vol. I. *Longmans,* NY: Green, 1954; pp. 682-85. Personality, immortality.

Neihardt, John. *Black Elk Speaks: Being the Story of the Oglala Sioux as Told to John G. Niehardt (Flaming Rainbow) 1881-1973.* NY: William Morrow, 1932. History of a spiritual American Indian.

Noyes, R., Jr. The Experience of Dying. *Psychiatry,* 1972; 35:174-84. See also "Near-Death Experiences: Their Interpretation and Significance." *Between Life And Death,* R. Kastenbaum (ed.). NY: Springer, 1974. Medical slant.

Noyes, R., and R. Kletti. "Depersonalization in the Face of Life-Threatening Danger: A Description." *Psychiatry,* 1976; 39:19-27. Survival techniques.

Osis, K. *Deathbed Observations by Physicians and Nurses.* NY: Parapsychology Foundation, 1961. Spiritual experiences just before death.

Osis, Karlis, Ph.D. and Haraldsson, Erlender, Ph.D. *At the Hour of Death.* NY: Hastings House Publishers, 1986. Spiritual experiences just before death.

Pinkwater, Daniel. *The Afterlife Diet.* Random House. NY: 1995. Humor, if you need a clue. "Weight-loss fiction."

Provonsha, J. *Is Death For Real: An Examination of Reported Near-Death Experiences in the Light of the Resurrection.* Boise, ID:Pacific Press, 1981. Skeptical inquiry.

Rawlings, Maurice. *Beyond Death's Door* and *To Hell and Back.* Nashville, TN: Thomas Nelson, 1993. Fundamentalist slant on the NDE.

Ring, Kenneth, Ph.D. *Life at Death.* NY: Quill, 1982. Basic book in the subject, the first research into NDE's.

Ring, Kenneth, Ph.D. *Heading Toward Omega: Human Evolution in an Ecological Age.* NY: Harper & Row, 1982. Inquiries about evolutionary patterns. See also Near-Death Experiences. Hastenbaum, R., and B. Kastenbaum. *Encyclopedia on Death.* Phoenix, AZ: Oryx Press, 1989 and *The Omega Project: Near-Death Experiences, UFO Encounters and Mind At Large.* Quill, 1992 for similarities between near-death experiences and alien abduction tales with aftereffects and psychological patterns.

Ritchie, George G. *Return From Tomorrow.* Waco, TX: Chosen Books 1978 and *My Life After Dying.* Norfolk, VA: Hampton Roads, 1991. Autobiographical.

Robbins, D. V. *Embarrassed by the Light: A Terminal Death Experience.* Raven House, 1995. A paroody of near-death experiences revealing what it feels like to be terminally dead.

Rogo, D. Scott. *The Return From Silence: A Study of Near-Death Experiences.* NY: Harper & Row, 1990. NDE research results for general readers.

Sabom, Michael. *Recollections of Death.* NY: Harper & Row, 1982. Cardiologist who examined his beliefs only to accept the NDE as a legitimate.

Sagan, Carl. *Broca's Brain:Reflections on the Romance of Science, Broccoli and Old Lace.* NY: Random House, 1979. NDE's as recreated birth memories.

St. John of the Cross(translated, edited with intro by E. Allison Peers from the critical edition of Silverio de Santa Teresa 1542-1591. *Neche Oscura del Alma -The Dark Night of the Soul).* NY: Image Books, Doubleday, 1991. Trauma prior to mystical conversion experiences.

St. Theresa of Avila (translated and edited by E. Allison Peers from the critical edition of P. Silverio de Santa Teresa. *The Interior Castle).* Garden City, NY: Image Books, 1961.

Schucman, Helen. *A Course in Miracles.* Tiburea, CA: Viking, 1995. Focuses on principles of universal love and forgiveness with a revelatory impact on people of many faiths.

Sharp, Kimberly Clark. *After The Light.* NY: William Morrow, 1995. Autobiographical.

Sullivan, Lawrence (ed.) *Death, Afterlife and the Soul.* NY: Macmillan, 1989. Religion, history and culture - comparative studies.

Sutherland, Cherie. *Transformed By The Light: Life After Near-Death Experiences.* NY: Bantam, 1992. General information from an Australian author.

Sutherland, Cherie. *Within The Light. NY: Bantam Books, 1995.* NDE experience.

Tart, Charles (ed. by Charles T. Tart). *Altered States of Consciousness.* San Francisco, CA: Harper, 1990.Altered states of consciousness.

Twemlow, S. et al. "The Out-of-Body Experience: A Phenomenological Typology based on Questionaire Responses." American Journal of Psychiatry, 1982; 139:450-55.

Taittiriya Upanishad (transl. by F. Max Müler), Section 4.1, Black Yajur Veda. NY: Dover Publications, 1962. Early Hindu sacred books and Sprituality.

Vicchio, S. "Near-Death Experiences: A Critical Review of the Literature and Questions for Further Help." *Anabiosis: The Journal for Near-Death Studies*, 1981; 1:66-87

Vincent, Ken R. *Visions of God From the Near-Death Experience*. Burdett, NY: Larson Publications, 1994. Comparison of NDE's with mystical conversion experiences.

Wilson, Ian. *The After-Death Experience - The Physics of the Non-Physical*. NY: William Morrow & Co., 1989."Future life."

Zaleski, Carol. *Otherworld Journeys: Accounts of Near-Death Experiences in Medieval and Modern Times*. NY: Oxford University Press, 1995. A look at the same experience in different times.

Note: Current information can be monitored through the Journal of Near-Death Studies and Vital Signs, both quarterly, available with membership to IANDS, the International Association of Near-Death Studies, Inc. P.O. Box 502, East Windsor Hill, CT 06028-0502 USA (203) 528-4144.

# Index

Please send me _____ additional copies of **When Ego Dies: A Compilation of Near-Death and Mystical Conversions Experiences** at $9.95 per book. Add $4.00 a book for priority shipping. Texas residents add 8.25% sales tax. Immediate shipment guaranteed.

Note: 15% discount for purchases of 5-9 books. 20% discount for purchases of 10 or more books. Resellers please call for wholesale discount information.

Name: _____ Firm: _____

Address (no P.O. box): _____

City: _____ State:_____ Zip: _____

Telephone: _____

Payment:

___ Check or money order enclosed.

Visa or MC Account#: _____

Exp. Date _____ Signature: _____

**Emerald Ink Publishing • 7141 Office City Drive Suite 220 •Houston, TX 77087**

Please send _____ gift copies of **When Ego Dies: A Compilation of Near-Death and Mystical Conversions Experiences** at $9.95 per book. Add $4.00 a book for priority shipping. Texas residents add 8.25% sales tax. Immediate shipment guaranteed.

Ship to: Name: _____ Firm:_____

Address (no P.O. box): _____

City: _____ State:_____ Zip: _____

Telephone: _____

Ship to: Name: _____ Firm:_____

Address (no P.O. box): _____

City: _____ State:_____ Zip: _____

Telephone: _____

Ship to: Name: _____ Firm:_____

Address (no P.O. box): _____

City: _____ State:_____ Zip: _____

Telephone: _____

Payment:

___ Check or money order enclosed.

Visa or MC Account#: _____

Exp. Date _____ Signature: _____

**Emerald Ink Publishing • 7141 Office City Drive Suite 220 •Houston, TX 77087**